Speech of the Unknown Future

JOHN C. WOODCOCK

ISBN: 1530496837
ISBN-13: 978-1530496839

D EDICATION

"Who is the awe-inspiring guest who knocks at our door so portentously?"

C. G. Jung

C ONTENTS

ACKNOWLEDGMENTS

1. *Cover graphic*: New Grange (1905), public domain.
2. *Bollingen high-relief*: © Dennis L. Merritt. (2012): The Cry of Merlin: Jung, the Prototypical Ecopsychologist. Fisher King Press. http://www.fisherkingpress.com.

P REFACE

There is today a surfeit of cultural practices, oriented towards the *posited* future, that merely reflect personal beliefs or desires, or are utopian or, as we know through terrorism, are destructive in character.

We can turn to sport, business, and politics, for example. The athlete is trained to mentally hold a picture of victory before her while she works to "catch up" to that image in her actual performance. Business acts on the basis of trends and futurists such as Faith Popcorn make a lot of money from accurately "forecasting" the future, or identifying "sweeping societal movements, or emerging consumer patterns." She has been called the Nostradamus of marketing. Politics takes action on the basis of a constructed imagination of the future, particularly "worst case scenarios," often making that imagination materialize in ways that nobody expects or wants.

But *all* of these practices are based on pasting an already-formed picture of the future, like a decal, *on top of* the unknown future, and then acting in ways to concretize that picture as the agreed-upon reality. These widespread practices of addressing the future impose a constructed "world" picture on the unknown future, supporting global cultural practices that spring from the forms of knowledge acquired from positing the "reality" status of that preferred picture.

This traditional and trusted method of addressing the future has the calamitous effect of leaving us totally unprepared when the *unknown* future unfolds in a way that does not conform to that picture—the picture that was understood as the real future. We name this situation as "the end of the world," because cultural practices built on a posited "preferred future" lose all meaning when confronted with the determining power of the Real. One powerful example of such an impending collapse lies in the frantic efforts to keep the financial system going according the preferred outcome of growth or profit maximization, while the empirical resources that support such a picture of the future run out.

Positing a picture of the future, as *the* future, seems to guarantee the preferred outcomes but this is not working any more. A chasm has opened up between our preferred "world picture" (taken as the real world) and the unknown future (the Real).

We now need another way to address the future, the

future in its character of being always unknown and yet REAL! *This* future requires a corresponding method, a cultural practice that synchronizes to the quality of the future as unknown yet real, and at the same time participates in its coming-to-be.

This book is an attempt to "spell out" such a method. In Part One, I point to a new form of literature that is emerging into visibility. This "form" looks chaotic and threatening when judged from the perspective of our traditional consciousness which has stabilized over centuries of habituated thought structures—"frozen" polarities such as: inner/outer; self/other; fictional/empirical; past/future; psychological/literary, as well as the fundamental law of contradiction.

The new form embodies the breakdown of these stabilizing categories and anyone practicing this method, as I show in Part One, will feel the threatening chaos to the point of madness. I say this because the breakdown has already happened. It is already logically "behind" us and those individuals who are attuned to this breakdown are subjected to its necessity, and begin to participate in and express its violent processes of transformation.

But is chaos all there is to "find" in this new art form? In Part Two, I present examples of this "mad" writing. I want to show that, within the chaos of a complete category breakdown (i.e., a transformation in consciousness), *something else* may be discerned! But this *other* cannot be named as a present *thing* because all such named things or appearances belong to the past (i.e., as

3

already given to us in their being). This unknown *other* can however be discerned indirectly through the hint, the unexpected intrusion, the unintended detail, the peripheral, the anomaly, the accidental. As well as privileging these phenomena, the "artist" must also valorize soul qualities such as uncertainty, receptivity to the unknown, surrender of self-interest, letting go of attachment to any egoic position, and a courageous willingness to enter the chaos of the unknown.[1]

This new cultural practice prepares the "artist" as a mouthpiece for the unknown future in its character as *other*. Only this cultural practice can express, by hint and suggestion, the emerging unknown future, or as Jung poetically puts it, the awe-inspiring guest. This practice is thus an "artistic" *act* that begins to unfold the unknown future into actuality.

If the essays in Part Two are "successful" as mouthpieces for the unknown future, then the reader may take up the hints offered by them and like-wise choose to participate, through resonant poetic or artistic action, in welcoming the coming guest, the unknown future.

There may be a question, why this particular cultural practice? Why not let the future arrive "on its own"? Why are we needed to "participate in the unfolding of some "unknown future"? What's wrong with simply *positing* a future (having goals, aspirations, etc.) and then striving to attain it? This important question has occupied my attention for many years and my books go into considerable detail about it. In a nutshell, we always already participate in the appearances, at least when they

4

are appearing ("discovered") for the "first time", i.e., before they stabilize into familiar things or objects through habitual use of language. This *unconscious* participation is of no cultural concern during relatively stable times when established knowledge or generally accepted perceptions of reality can afford to ignore the anomaly.

We are now living in a time where anomalies (new, living ideas—*novelty*), are breaking through into the personal imagination of individuals at an accelerating rate, often unfolding into actuality through minds that have already succumbed to the twin aspects of power and control that these ideas bring with them. We are thus already participating, albeit unconsciously, in unfolding a possible unknown future, and it is beginning to take on terrifying features and proportions.

We can no longer ignore the fact of our participation in actualizing any possible, unknown future. We should examine our seducibility to power and control and the role that seducibility plays in the outcome. We should grasp the fact that, after all, power and control, as autonomous factors in the psyche, do not have our human interests under consideration. We can then ask if it is possible to choose, to make a decision about *how* we are to participate.

The nascent cultural practice that I tentatively call "mouthpiece" is a way of being oriented to the unknown future, a way that does not involve unconscious identification with power or control, but instead is a way of love and humility, with a gesture of hospitality towards the coming guest.

---

[1] By "art" and "artist", I am referring to a practice that discloses the new Being (the unknown future). The artist in this sense participates, willingly or not, in Life's seeking to create a distance from the burden of its own suffering (Nietzsche, Heidegger, Henry).

PART ONE: APPROACHING THE UNKNOWN FUTURE

We approach the unknown future by way of "catastrophe". Within this word lie images of turning, like the vortex, or whirlwind, with the added inflection of turning down, ruination, conclusion. Most surprisingly, buried deep with the root *cat-*, lies a meaning of giving birth in the sense that many animals give birth standing up, dropping their young to the ground. Before the unknown future emerges into full visibility, chaos will gain full ascendancy. This chaotic process at first takes the form of a necessary psychological break down as certain individuals "get wind of" the coming changes. This catastrophe is, at bottom, a breakdown in hardened categories of thought, as reflected in language. As these collapse, the individual is thrown into chaos. Her stable world disappears.[1] Tremendous, potent energies are released—the energies of *living language*! This "linguistic furor" destroys categories reified over centuries of habitual use of language, giving us our stable world of appearances—categories such as inner/outer, self/other, past/future, and so on.

Individuals who approach the unknown future must enter this whirlwind, and those who can hang onto their sanity often bring forth expressions of the chaos by way of a new art form, as we will see.

I have been writing for thirty-five years or so. I have written thirteen books now, many articles and essays, and poetry. I have also created some works of art. I keep a dream journal and have countless notebooks. I have also completed a master's degree and doctoral degree, both of which required years of putting pen to paper, or finger to keyboard.

Only in my academic writing did I receive some formal training but I still do not know how to type beyond the two-fingered method. In all my other literary output, I received no training or coaching in the craft of writing. I simply do not conceive of my life as an author. I do not consider the craft of writing as a career for me. I apparently picked up what I needed in order to say what I wanted to say, as I went along. When, finally, some kind individuals agreed to edit a small piece or two, I was shocked at the degree to which their careful editing exposed holes in my knowledge of grammar, spelling, punctuation, structural convention, formatting styles, etc.

Why then do I write at all?

One reason to write of course is to show others that you know what they know, i.e. to communicate your intellectual readiness to enter a community dedicated to a particular discipline. In this kind of writing, the personality or psychology of the author is not a topic. Instead, the writer must rise up to the level of the "theoretical 'I'" that is, the voice of the discipline itself. Personal opinions or feelings are not wanted here. This intellectual demand is well captured in the requirement that the author write in the 3rd person or with the "I" of the discipline, and to produce citations wherever epistemological claims are made. Originality is not a requirement as much as familiarity with the already given body of knowledge. The granting of a degree is the public sign that the individual has reached the intellectual standards set by the discipline.

Another reason to write concerns the craft of writing. An author may spend years developing and refining her craft, excelling at a genre for example. The author's personality remains relevant here in the sense that we, the readers, can recognize the signature of the literary work. For example, Isaac Asimov's signature, within the genre of Science Fiction novels, is readily discernible.

There is yet another reason to write, one that has nothing to do with access to a body of knowledge or allegiance to an art form or genre of literature. I came across a vivid example of this "reason to write" in a movie, *Quills* (2000), which in part concerns the penmanship of the Marquis de Sade (Jeffrey Rush). He is imprisoned in an attempt to control his literary output, but pen and ink are smuggled in; when these are removed, de Sade uses wine and blood as ink; when these are denied, he uses his own shit to smear words on walls, etc. We can see from this example that another reason to write is because one is compelled to, with no regard for conventions, established genres, or anything else for that matter. The writer is seized!

I write because something is happening to me that forces me to write. My body heats up in an inflammatory reaction that can only be quenched, at least partially, by writing a process going on "within"—not writing *about* a process going on "within" but *writing* it as it is happening.

My early books express this process in detail and I was too immersed to ask the question, "What am I doing, what kind of writing is this? Is it a genre of writing, or at least the beginnings of one?" I simply wrote. The fact that I could eventually ask this question, however, is a signal that, to some extent, the process was becoming conscious of itself and thus reflective. One of my early attempts to conceptualize the kind of writing I was doing appears this way:[2]

> I begin by paying attention to certain events occurring in the world: i.e. events characterized by qualities of the unusual, the unfamiliar, the startling, all of which obviously involve my psychological participation, and then I open myself up to these phenomena sufficiently for them to penetrate my consciousness, so that I begin to *think the thought* of the phenomenon, as distinct from my thinking *about* them This process is in effect an initiation into another form of consciousness, the consciousness of the phenomenon. This finally can form the basis for new action in the world, action that is not simply a repeat of the known past but instead carries the germ of a new future. These actions always take me away from the security of the familiar into the unknown future.
>
> My method of writing is therefore an attempt to develop an art form that can demonstrate this process. I soften the boundaries of my ego and pay attention to unusual, unfamiliar, or even startling, images that "arrive". I take up a relationship with these visitors and am prepared to leave my present path to follow their hints. I

record this process as it goes on. A kind of wandering therefore takes place in my writing, as in my life.

In this way, I move from a memory, to a dream, to a reflection of an event in the world, to an etymological study of a word, to the words of another author. I do not concern myself with any separation between inner and outer, past and future, fact and fiction i.e. the usual categories of experience. The one constant is that all my writing springs out of the soil of immediate experience and so is real. I pay attention to detail, or hints that emerge freely from "within", no matter how small or seemingly insignificant. It takes a kind of surrender to psychic process in order to write this way, and a faith that I won't fall merely into chaos, or madness. But this is far from certain!

This conception helped as I began to understand that the nature of my writing involved, not any genre or established craft, but a breakdown of such categories, and indeed, a breakdown of fundamental categories such as mechanical space and linear past, present, and future, those very categories that constitute the background of our stabilized modern structure of consciousness. This early formulation distinguishes what I had believed was merely a personal breakdown from an objective breakdown of categories occurring "in the background" of modern consciousness. This real process at present has no category with which to name and therefore grasp it, since it involves a *breakdown* in categories. I could use names like "fictional", or "imaginal", but these categories come loaded with a history that has deprived them of any truth or reality. In fact these words currently mean the opposite—not real, fantasy, entertainment only, falsity, etc.

But the phenomenology is conclusive. This process is real and has no referent outside itself. For example a breakdown of categories does not refer outside itself to a literal break down on a personal level or to the scale of a literal world catastrophe, although many people who are caught up in these background movements often make these misinterpretations. And yet, because this movement is the background or the "within-ness" of the real world, then it follows that madness or world catastrophe are not to be excluded after all.

How can we understand the necessity of this contradiction?

An example may help us here. C. G. Jung had a series of "world catastrophe" visions just prior to the outbreak of the First World War. In his book *Memories, Dreams, Reflections* he offers two contradictory interpretations.[3] Being an experienced psychiatrist he understood psychosis very well and at first he suspected one was menacing him. But when the war broke out he began wonder instead how his personal inner experiences could have something to do with associated events in the real world (the catastrophe of the war). This question of the connection between inner psychic events and outer events in the world became a lifetime's work for Jung, and is no less important and perhaps no more understood today.

For the next several years following his visions, Jung

was caught up in psychic processes that involved a breakdown of categories such as inner and outer, and he went through a very real personal breakdown that simulated psychosis (auditory hallucinations, talking to invisible figures, extreme emotional states etc.) but, unlike madness, Jung's ego remained intact. He was able to reflect upon, as well as undergo the breakdown of categories.

The written record of this journey is now published as The Red Book.[4] Jung's understanding of what he went through is complex and beyond the scope of this book, but we can touch on two aspects that are relevant here.[5] On the one hand, after Jung emerged from his immersion in the "breakdown", he returned to the categories of inner and outer and took up the question of how one could have anything to do with the other. For example, his theory of synchronicity is a sustained attempt to find a theoretical connection between inner events, say a dream, and a "coincidental" event in the outer world.

On the other hand, Jung seemed to accept the breakdown of categories (e. g. spatial and temporal categories that form the structure of modern consciousness) and to change accordingly in his self-definition. He thus became *initiated* by the experiences themselves into a new form of consciousness and reality. This initiation gave Jung the power to form new conceptions appropriate to this reality and thus perceive new appearances of the real world. These new conceptions also gave rise to his unique notion of soul as absolute interiority—a conception subsequently fully developed by Wolfgang Giegerich.[6]

Jung's complex and contradictory responses to the "breakdown of categories", have given rise to conflicting theoretical and methodological paths within the Jungian community but may be sympathetically understood as the result of a pioneer's attempt to face the sheer terror of participating in a breakdown of the very categories that support modern consciousness and its correlative reality. And, if consciousness itself is undergoing a transformation, then personal breakdowns and world convulsions are certain, as our history demonstrates so well.[7]

One significant category breakdown is that of doing and reflection. Within our modern structure of consciousness we consider these a pair of opposites. We can do something in life or reflect on something in life but not both at the same time.

In the kind of writing I am suggesting it seems that both happen simultaneously or something else happens that subsumes both within it. I call this "happening" *participation*. Participation with the background process of category breakdown is reflection and doing, yet neither. Thus, participation can be sharply distinguished from automatic writing where the writer's consciousness plays no part. It is also different from having an experience and subsequently writing about that experience from memory. The writing that emerges from this participatory process therefore is a form (it's probably too early to call it a genre) that *embodies* such category breakdowns (inner/outer, past/present/future, self/other, action/reflection, even psychology/literature, etc.)

To this extent such writing will appear crazy, as writers of this emerging form are forced to express mind-bending notions that are faithful to the phenomenon yet incoherent when subjected to the requirements of our stable modern form of consciousness.

I recently saw an example of such "nonsense" when I was awake, late at night, unable to sleep. I turned on the TV and to my surprise saw a re-run of Terminator (1984). The heroine (Sarah) and her rescuer are being chased by the Terminator and are resting in a tunnel where she seeks to understand the logic of what is happening. The machines had sent a Terminator back through time to kill her so that she cannot give birth to the hero and then train him in warfare to save future humanity from the machines. The mere presence of this future machine forces this simple waitress to gain the very skills that the machines fear, and to become pregnant with the "saviour". Her rescuer had previously been arrested and a forensic psychologist listened to his story of travel from the future in order to save Sarah from the machine. He declared the prisoner completely delusional. The heroine, however, is willing to listen, as he talks, not of futures, but *possible futures*. From their point of view, now in the present, they are confronted with possible futures penetrating the present (in the form of the Terminator who is only *one* possible future) and their actions matter, although they cannot predict the outcome (whether Sarah would be killed or not).

It seems from this and other similar examples that the idea of possible futures intersecting with the present and demanding action, without knowing the outcome, becomes important only when the usual categories that support present-day consciousness break down.

There are many such instances of art forms now that are "speaking" this way and seem to be engaging the contemporary artistic mind. One such book is the compelling The Exegesis of Philip K. Dick, which is a partial collection of the "mad" writings of science-fiction writer, Phillip K. Dick, (Blade Runner, The Minority Report).[8] This book gives us a glimpse of his eight years-long immersion into the background of consciousness as long-held categories break down.

In 1974, Dick had a revelation that ignited a superhuman feat of writing constantly over a long series of nights, running to eight thousand pages, a "sudden, discorporating slippage into vast and total knowledge that he would spend the rest of his life explicating, or exegeting."[9] The posthumous publication of some of these texts highlights Dick's long and arduous attempt to understand what exactly was happening to him, in a similar manner to C. G. Jung's efforts, as recorded in his The Red Book. I can choose any page at random to get a feel for sheer movement taking place, on-rushing fervour, a furore, gathering rapids, as punctuation breaks down, or ceases really to matter, as an onrushing life begins to prevail. It's like navigating a maelstrom at times, with little islands emerging only to be swept away again. The structure of that book is described as "a freewheeling voice that ranges through personal confession, esoteric scholarship, dream accounts, and fictional figures… one of the most improbable and mind-altering manuscripts ever brought to light."[10]

When I compared this description of Dick's writing with that of my own (see above), I knew that we had some common ground. I also had endured a prolonged "meltdown" in which the very categories that support our present-day consciousness dissolved. I was also forced to write my way out of it, and then I learned the way out is *via* the way in. I had to participate more deeply in the material that was presenting itself to me, as Dick had to, as well.

A key methodological approach in producing this kind of "mad" writing is that the author takes seriously whatever phenomenon presents itself, *in its own terms*. The author must be able to remain "within" the phenomenon long enough so that it can teach her what it means in terms of its own logic, no matter how crazy it may sound when appraised from the categories of our current form of consciousness. The author is thus compelled to think self-presentational thoughts that defy rationality. I'll give one example here from Dick's book, Valis, which I read with enormous enthusiasm:

Dick tells us of a dream he had in which he is living with this wife:[11]

> I have had dreams of another place myself, a lake up north and the cottages and small rural houses north and the cottages and small rural houses around its south shore. In my dream I arrive there from Southern California, where I live; this is a vacation spot, but it is very old-fashioned. All the houses are wooden, made of the brown shingles so popular in California before World War Two. The roads are dusty. The cars are older, too.

Following the dream, which Dick accepts completely in its own terms, he begins to compare its reality with his waking life, which does not include many of the elements in the dream. He then gets a memory of his father and realizes that in his dream he is living his father's life. From this achievement, Dick argues further that the individual psyche contains the history not only of her personal life but of our entire race, back to its origins, back to the stars: "This is gene pool memory, the memory of the DNA."

Dick's theory of history has been discovered and articulated by others. In modern times, C. G. Jung has developed a unique view of history which is very close to Dick's, namely that we are psychologically the "outcome" of many historical transformations in consciousness, all of which may be reconstructed in our modern minds, with the correct methodology—history, as much as it is psychologically relevant to our lives, may be found "within".[12] The really significant point here that I want to make is that Dick did not gain this knowledge externally, as a student of psychology might do so. He was *initiated* into it by the phenomenon—his dream, which he took to be as real as his waking life! His eyes were opened to another reality!

To take this line of argument a step further, we can ask what ultimately happens if, when the very categories that support our current form of consciousness break down, we stay immersed in the chaos that logically follows, as Dick does and as I did (in my case for about fifteen years or so). The process at first becomes mad and both *Exegesis* and *Valis* feel that way, from the perspective of our modern-day consciousness. But Dick emerges with an astounding conclusion—one that I am totally in agreement with, on the basis of my own mad immersion: Dick discovered that a reversal in a fundamental polarity takes place.

He shows us that if we take madness seriously and in a sustained way; if we take it on its own terms, as it presents itself to us, then a fundamental polarity that has driven our Western culture for thousands of years, giving rise, finally to our modern structure of consciousness—the rational/irrational polarity succumbs and reverses itself!

Astounding!

Dick outlines this reversal in his cosmogony:[13]

> The single most striking realization that Fat [Dick's fictional "I"] had come to was his concept of the universe as irrational and governed by an irrational mind, the creator deity. If the universe were taken to be rational, not irrational, then something breaking into it might seem irrational, since it would not belong. But Fat, having reversed everything, saw the rational breaking into the irrational. The immortal plasmate had invaded our world and the plasmate was totally rational, whereas our world is not.

What this means for us is this: The stability of our world has, up to modern times, assured us of our sanity. Now this stability is undermining itself with the consequence that all such assurance is gone and we may well now be insane, according to Dick. Our modern consciousness has so far isolated itself from everything else (the private self) that it is now psychotic—yet, of course, it thinks of itself as totally sane. Furthermore those aspects of our psychological being, now *persona non grata*—dreams, visions, "accidents", etc.—are the harbours of the very sanity that can cure us of the insanity of psychological isolation.

This is also my conclusion, based on many years of immersion in "madness", and taking them every bit as seriously as Philip K. Dick does, until I realized that the madness was now the new sanity.

Dick's way of writing demands both reflection and doing, i.e., what I earlier called participation! The ability of the author to engage this way probably determines the extent to which he could legitimately be called mad. The doing is a needing to act without knowing the outcome in the sense that modern consciousness knows (subject-object knowing). If we know the outcome then obviously we are merely repeating the past in some way, since present-day consciousness *knows* only in terms of the past (memory). This "doing" can at first be frightening to those who feel the "demand" to act in this way. Yet one can get used to it and even become curious.

If we participate with possible futures as they penetrate the present, does it matter *how* we act in relation to them? If it did not matter then we would be forced to acknowledge a deterministic universe or an "intelligent designer", but "possible futures" more speaks of a dark urge that agitates, burrows, seeking to "get ahead" or to enter material reality by finding any available opening. Philosophically we could talk of this process as a union of teleology and contingency. Wounded individuals, like me, are such available openings and the dark urge simply enters. It is up to the individual to survive the onslaught as the "burrowing spirit" works its way into the world. And it is up to the individual to develop those soul capacities that will assist the actualization of possible futures in forms that support biological and cultural life, rather than destroy it. There are many casualties of this impersonal process and the record of such encounters constitutes culture in its many varied forms.[14]

The impersonal nature of the burrowing spirit was brought home to me by a dream I had many years ago. In this dream:

> I am on a winding road in the country. I see a young woman throwing a boomerang in a field and it comes my way. I pick it up and throw it. This attracts her and she comes my way and joins me. We go by some animals and see a calf split off from the herd, alone and bleating for its mother. It is near a snake. The cobra rears up and it is golden and climbs easily onto the calf's back. The calf can barely take the weight and can do no more than try not to collapse.

This dream frightened me.

The snake, as the burrowing spirit, when it enters the world, must rest on a foundation (serpent wrapped around the world, or egg, on a turtle's back, tree etc.). But these animal aspects, as psychological realities, are today the most undeveloped aspects of the consciousness that gives rise to our modern Western culture and thus, the psychological foundation is weak. D. H. Lawrence is one modern writer who saw this issue but could offer only a literalized solution to it. He was not able to see it as a psychological problem involving the deepest levels of our modern consciousness.

It appears that the future of our species depends on a certain spiritual development to take place quickly, perhaps too quickly for the human participant. This unpreparedness in the human recipient appears as images of the young, weak, wounded, and immature. A huge transformation in consciousness is taking place, supported on a relatively weak base. Such a structure generates a feeling, on the human level, of being too young, bearing too much responsibility, being abandoned or let down by parents, left to assume responsibilities that one is not prepared for. Picasso's Minotauromachy pictures this precarious situation—the monster approaches civilization and everyone flees except a young girl who stands to meet him, with a light in one hand and some flowers in the other.

All these features appears in my dream, as it does in Dick's *Valis* where the protagonist, Horselover Fat, is paired with feminine figures who are dying, ill, frail, and in need of "rescuing", unable to cope. In my case, although the situation was dire, there was also the possibility, within the image of the calf, of a mighty bull, which can easily support the serpent. I held onto that possibility for many years as I slowly learned to assume the burden of the cobra.[15] The impersonal nature of the burrowing spirit can easily be seen in the fact that the calf was not special in any way. It simply met the criteria needed for the burrowing spirit to "get in" i.e., alienation, isolation, neediness, and, therefore, availability.

I am now reminded of a little book that Owen Barfield wrote, in which he encounters his version of the burrowing spirit in the form of an invisible angelic visitor (the Meggid) with whom Barfield enters discussions. At the very end of the book, Burgeon (Barfield's literary ego) asks the Meggid why the angel chooses him. The Meggid answers simply:[16]

> Have you supposed you are the only one? There are others, whom you will find, if you have not done so already ... The two holocausts have touched you comparatively lightly, the reigns of terror not at all ... Many would have been reached before you [but for the holocausts]. The area of our choice at present is not so wide.

The stability of our current reality has been based on habits of thought that keep the opposites apart: inner/outer, past/future, subject/object, self/other, to name just a few. We have slowly acquired knowledge of beings, based on the stability of these paired opposites. From this knowledge we have built cultural forms and practices (ways of being) that essentially tell us who we are in an unquestioned world. Maintaining these opposites in place requires tremendous energy in the form of will. Now that they are breaking down, this energy is getting released and catching receptive human beings in its power. Once again the Meggid teaches Burgeon:

> Your brothers in the West will learn, indeed they are beginning to suspect already that within each of them, deep hidden and hitherto unconscious, there lives a fury of destructive force, beside which the destructive forces in nature pale. [17]

This energy is the energy of what I have called elsewhere, living language, once released from its imprisonment in habitual forms of thought (categories).[18] This release of living language appears at first, as Barfield says, "like a fury of destructive force", or as Emerson says:[19]

> The things we now esteem fixed shall, one by one, detach themselves, like ripe fruit, from our experience, and fall. The wind shall blow them none knows whither. The landscapes, the figures, Boston, London, are facts as fugitive as any institution past, or any whiff of mist or smoke, and so is society, and so is the world. The soul looketh steadily forwards, creating a world before her, leaving worlds behind her. She has no dates, nor rites, nor persons, nor specialties, nor men. The soul knows only the soul; the web of events is the flowing robe in which she is clothed.

Jung called it a lava flow or incandescent:[20]

> I hit upon this stream of lava, and the heat of its fires reshaped my life. That was the primal stuff which compelled me to work upon it, and my works are a more or less successful endeavor to incorporate this incandescent matter into the contemporary picture of the world.

I could add here my own experience of the destructive power of living language:[21]

> My symptoms reach an unbearable peak tonight and I dream... the bomb: I am to suffer and endure consciously the effects of the heat and radiation of a thermonuclear bomb. It goes off near me and I feel the heat in my blood and it pours out of my mouth. The heat is tremendous. It was also extremely sexual.

As Emerson says, living language, once released from its historical fetters, seeks, in its fury, to destroy habitual forms of thought, or the institutional mind. It is a terrifying experience that, at the same time, is joyful.[22] This breakdown, and release of enormous destructive and life-giving energies is now upon us. Just last night, I dreamed of a huge, whirlwind storm emerging into visibility from a mountain and approaching us. Its self-originating light is partially obscured by a circus that is in the foreground—i.e. obscured by the artificial lights of the circus. Yet the storm itself *is* becoming visible. After the dream I immediately thought of the Trump circus which, at this time, has gripped the American imagination. The establishment (or institutional mind) can only understand this eruption in terms of the past (e.g. comparing Trump to Hitler, fascism, demagoguery, etc.) while, as the political drama deepens, fear is increasing because these categories of the past simply cannot grasp what is happening: a storm is coming and that storm is also called the coming guest, i.e. the unknown future.[23]

As my dream suggests, the possibility of perceiving the storm, *in its own terms*, has now arrived. Some of us may not be so seduced by "the circus" that we do see anything else happening in the deeper background. Those that do see the deeper background are in a position to become mouthpieces for that background, as it emerges into actuality. What will these mouthpieces "say", or rather can we perceive this background at work through whatever these mouthpieces say or, better, through whatever art form they choose to say it.

In the essays that follow, I will try to give some hints of what to look for in identifying a possible mouthpiece for the unknown future. If we can recognize the phenomenology of the coming guest, then we are better situated to *welcome* "him", rather than refusing the guest through terrified reactions, as is happening worldwide today.

---

[1] See my books, The Imperative and Mouthpiece for an account of my own experience of "breakdown".

[2] Woodcock, J. C. (2012). Living in Uncertainty Living with Spirit. Bloomington. iUniverse. 77.

[3] Jung, C. G. (1963). Memories, Dreams, Reflections. New York: Random House. 175 ff.

[4] Jung, C. G. (2009). The Red Book. (S. Shamdasani, Ed., S. Shamdasani, M. Kyburz, & J. Peck, Trans.) New York: W.W. and Norton & Company.

[5] For a detailed analysis, see Giegerich, W. (2010). "Liber Novis, that is, The New Bible, A First Analysis of C. G. Jung's Red Book". Spring 83, 361-413.

[6] See, for example, Giegerich, W. (2012). What is Soul? New Orleans. Spring Journal Inc.

[7] For a detailed analysis of this process see Woodcock, J. C. (2013). Overcoming Solidity: World Crisis and the New Nature. Bloomington. iUniverse.

[8] Dick, P. K. (2011). The Exegesis of Philip K. Dick. (P. L. Jackson, Ed.) New York: Houghton Mifflin Harcourt.

[9] From the Introduction.

[10] From the Flyleaf.

[11] Dick, P. K. (2010-04-18). Valis (S.F. MASTERWORKS). Orion. Kindle Edition. 113 ff.

[12] For a detailed discussion of this unique view of history see Giegerich, W. (2008). Soul Violence. New Orleans. Spring Journal.

[13] Dick, P. K. (2010-04-18). Valis (S.F. MASTERWORKS). Orion. Kindle Edition.) 112.

[14] For a fuller discussion of this aspect of individual participation, see Woodcock, J. C. (2013). Manifesting Possible Futures: towards a new genre of literature. Available at Amazon.

[15] For a fuller account, see Woodcock, J. C. (2011). The Imperative. Available at Amazon.

[16] Barfield, O. (1965). Unancestral Voice. Middletown. Wesleyan University Press.

[17] Barfield, O. Unancestral Voice. Middleton. Wesleyan University Press. 1965. 158.

[18] See my book, The Peril in Thinking (2015), available at Amazon.

[19] Emerson, R. W. The Oversoul.

[20] C. G. Jung. Memories, Dreams, Reflections.

[21] See my book, Mouthpiece. Available at Amazon.

[22] Nietzsche: "to realize in oneself the eternal joy of becoming—that joy which also encompasses joy of destruction." From The Twilight of the Gods.

[23] See my book, The Coming Guest and the New Art Form. Available at Amazon.

PART TWO: THE UNKNOWN FUTURE APPROACHING US

If you will contemplate your lack of fantasy, of inspiration and inner aliveness, which you feel as sheer stagnation and barren wilderness, and impregnated with the interest born of alarm at your inner death, then something can take shape in you, for your inner emptiness conceals just as great a fullness if only you will allow it to penetrate into you. If you prove receptive to this 'call of the wild,' the longing for fulfilment will quicken the sterile wilderness of your soul as rain quickens the dry earth.

(C. G. Jung)

Bethinking is the art of finding words, is poetic, the art of finding names, the art of naming being. An inherited word is adapted to the unique exigencies of a moment. What are the standards for judging an attempt at in-vention (bethinking)? Has it found its voice or theme? Has it learned to adapt itself to the new dimension that it itself has opened up?

(R. Polt)

FROM INTERPRETATION TO PARTICIPATION

In Part One I spoke of the unknown future approaching us in a storm of destructive fury, its intention being to "break up" hardened categories of thought, as reflected in our habitual language structures. In doing so tremendous "nuclear" energies are released, a flow starts up and a new form of language begins to self-present. This essay shows an example of this breakdown in established thought patterns, followed by a release of a "poetic", fluid, language that acts as a mouthpiece, giving us intimations of the unknown future.

It starts with some dreams.

Dream 1:

I awake in bed with a terrible pain in my belly. I fall into a half-sleep and learn that my step-father had been kicking and punching me while I was asleep, maybe sexual abuse too, while I was asleep. It's the violence that matters. I would often wake up in terrible pain but not knowing. My mother now tells me the reason. I am furious and leave home. I find my way to a school. I tell them my story and they say I can stay. A scene of sitting and eyes fill with tears while they go about their business. I tell them I am a teacher implying "hire me". One says they have just fired two teachers. I am shown my room—a library. They take out the table and I can stay in that space surrounded by books. I tell my mother who looks small and mousey to give me $10 000 so that I can leave. She agrees and leaves.

Dream 2:

Sigrid and I find our way back together after so many years. She welcomes me back but warns me that there is something very wrong with her womb and other organs. She is living alone in a small room with a cot. A friend asks if she is all right being with me. She says yes. She starts to tell me about her wound, how most of her adult life has been to try to heal herself medically. The details of hers and my history start to make sense and more is made explicit—her love, her reluctance, her shyness, her avoidance, disappearing from me, my lack of understanding. She also tells me that she has been composing music, poetry, in response to her wound. I get excited about this and ask to see some of it.

Dream 3:

A dream of complete loss, devastating loss. I force myself, a dream within the dream, to stay with the horror. My son and I are separated. He is in a strange place alone, no one to help. He is slowly going mad with isolation. I try to get to him but cannot. He finally is burned to death. J gives away all my clothes. I am shocked that she did that! I am totally without means. Nowhere to go, no way to earn money. Complete loss. I find myself at a farming community. They are holding an outdoor meeting. Someone is teaching the others. I stand a little behind and to the left of the speaker. I start to crumble. I am not going to make it. I can't do this any more. The pain is too great to stay with it, as I collapse to the ground.

Dream 4:

I dream that my son is leaving, going away I cannot stop him. Behind is the 'hateful mother', and I feel the force of her hatred towards me.

Four dreams! I cannot fixate on any one external interpretation (e.g. historical, childhood memory) because the memories are shifting, fluid, meaning uncertain. Did my stepfather, in fact, physically abuse me? My dream of separating from my own son who is then horribly burned to death in his mad isolation also has an historical component in that I had been painfully separated several times from my son over the years. When I was a small child my hateful mother separated me from my own father and successfully cut off all communication between us. My dream of "wounded Sigrid", also weaves in an historical person, Sigrid, who I knew and loved so many years ago. The dream figure belongs to a long series of such fictional appearances since that time of my youth. She is shown here in a state of isolation, cut off, and wounded, a purely "inner" story. Such a weaving of inner and outer realties, of historical fact and pure fiction! Surely a destruction of any too-easy interpretation, inner or outer is occurring in these dreams. Thinking is taking place, dream movement, certainly drawing from events in the world, but no longer only referring reductively back to them. Something new and unfamiliar is being said here, said in the sense of showing for the first time—an inception.

The question becomes: is it possible for me to say this new thinking? Is it possible for me to participate in its coming-to-be for the first time, in the sense that Polt means?

> In-vention is not planning or willing; it is a venturesome openness to an experience in which the artist himself may be transformed. It is neither the discovery of a previously formed object nor the creation *ex nihilo* of a form, but the attentive cultivation of meaning. It is neither a mere acceptance of the given nor an imposition that negates the given, but a creative reception of the given—an event of appropriation. In this way, in-vention undercuts the opposition between creativity and truth. It allows meaning to flourish—and allows the finder of meaning to flourish as well.[1]

The mood of my dreams is one of horror, pain, madness, and incredible violence, devastating loss—unbearable, yet I must bear it. I force myself to bear it—yes, a forceful *willing* to bear it!. And I can hear the dual meaning as one. I am both victim and perpetrator of the violence. As I do so, words come from within it, first from my dream mother who informs me of my stepfather's violence towards me. This knowledge leads me to where I must stay, in a room, surrounded by books. As I write this I begin to get glimmer of how one thread of my life has unfolded in the pursuit of knowledge, as I have tried to understand my own pain and suffering, conceived as such, i.e. as *my* pain, thanks to my dream mother's personalistic and concretistic interpretation. It seems that when we interpret our dreams reductively i.e. in terms of past empirical events, we are drawn into the pursuit of a form of knowledge, reason, that valorises the literal, the surface of events. The more we know the better, and the more the reality of the horror, and its violence remains occluded.

We thus ward off the abyss!

At the same time I am shown that the pain and woundedness does not belong to me in any empirical sense. It is the figure of Sigrid who is bearing it, in a state of isolation. She is now the wounded, isolated one, and I am shown to be in a state of ignorance, a complete lack of understanding. My inability to help (my son burned alive in mad isolation, trying for years to get medical help, the pursuit of knowledge) opens me up fully to the horror of isolation and its woundedness, as if to teach me that it is not a condition seeking a cure, or apotropaic healing. Instead, if this self-inflicted horror is endured to its fullest, without hope, then from out of this blind condition of pain, suffering, and death leaps poetry and music. As Heidegger says, "In life we make language work in a provisional way because we are signifying just superficial relations. Then comes up suddenly another language—that of the poetical."

And so, now, right now, suddenly the leap![2]

THE LEAP

art born from suffering borne
suffering of mad isolation
penetrating the vitals
sovereign domain of medical knowledge
now helpless and ignorant

how can the fictional penetrate the physical?
the ineluctable physical body?
the ineluctable fictional?
can we say this:
the physical wants to become fictional?
wants to speak?

picasso's mute minotaur
breaks into the civilised world
violent penetration
panic erupts
matador overcome
spear shatters

young girl
waiting for the mighty one
flowers and a candle, no more
the bull holds his hand out
against the piercing light
or reaching for it?
can she give him what he needs?
what can she offer?
flowers? light?
what can he take?

everything!

precarious moment

what does he seek?
driven mad in his bestial isolation
deep in the labyrinthine mind
he has now burst out
inarticulate bellow
physicality demanding speech
its speech
the speech of organs, blood, womb

the taming of the ox is done
finished

cultural catastrophe

he now returns in all his wildness
trapped no more in the deep recesses
of the cave beneath the civilised world

world destroyer

what is this new speech
this inception?
it is the bull-man's speech
wild, embodied, organic speech
speech that stirs the blood
opens organs
chorus of voices
not heard
for thousands of years
it begins …

---

[1] Polt, Richard. The Emergency of Being: On Heidegger's "Contributions to Philosophy". Kindle Edition.

[2] This poem suddenly leaped out of my musings—an inception!

NEW GRANGE: *ORIGINAL MOUTHPIECE*

Scholarship does not know definitively what the spirals at New Grange meant to the Celts.

They remain a mystery.

Scholars research the *outside* of this mystery, studying the empirical facts.

Is there a way *into* this 5000 year-old mystery, into an *experience* of this mystery? How can we have any experience of the past, i.e. of the *consciousness* of the past? There is a way—the way of living language. Modern words carry history within themselves and we call this linguistic history etymology. If we begin an etymological inquiry into words, allowing disciplined imagination to lead the way, then we can reach a place of inspiration where something *other* may penetrate our modern consciousness. This *other* is the consciousness or interiority of the past *and* a seed of the unknown future!

Inspiration!

Its very *sound* has a compelling pull on me. I hear my breath expel softly as the word is spoken. Its sound conveys breathing—mostly breath, with no hard consonant "stops".

So much like "whisper".

I look up its meaning although I already know that "spire" means to breathe.

"Spire" also has two other meanings: a single turn of a spiral and a tapering, rising to a point, like a church spire. All three meanings: breath, spiral, and tapering, are now independent of one another in our daily usage. But their meanings interpenetrate and echo one another in the sound of the word, "spiral".

An echo of the past? This preliminary "word work" already triggers a memory ...

Spirals and vortices have frequently appeared in my dreams over the years. Part of my subsequent research took me to the Celtic world where spirals of course play a prominent role. I learned that Celtic scholarship could not discover any definitive meaning for the many spirallic forms found on Celtic artifacts.

Now another memory surfaces, of an ancient rock carving depicting human figures with spirals emanating from their mouths! I saw it, I swear, yet to this day I cannot find any reference in the empirical world. I am left with the intriguing hint from memory that spirals and speech belong together, somehow.

But the archeological world of buried facts is not the only "portal" to our spiritual heritage—our dead past. It is also buried deep within our language, yes, as the past, but that past still *living* within our language, or as language's very within-ness.

I return to my word work.

In our modern language, as standardized by the dictionary, "spire" has three separate meanings, each seemingly unrelated to the others—all hidden within the word "inspiration".

Breathing seems so unrelated to spiraling and tapering.

I decide to dig more deeply into the living history of meanings residing in our everyday use of words.

A spire, as one turn of a spiral arises from *spira*, which

means to coil. A coil is a connected series of spirals, as in a coil of rope. "Coil" comes from *cooligere*, Latin for "collect". This makes sense since a coil, in collecting spires together, becomes a coil in the first place.

But then a surprise!

The word "collect" arises from the Latin *colligere* and this word emerges in turn from the etymological root, *leg-*. *Leg-*, as well as meaning to collect and gather, as in the Latin *legere*, from which one meaning of religion is derived—a sacred gathering, has a derivative meaning of "to speak", or *logos*.

Buried within the meaning of the word "inspiration" are meanings of breath, sacred gatherings, speech, spirals, and tapering to a point, as in a church steeple.
I have at last penetrated the historical depths of language to the forgotten psyche, the ancient *living* past, as reconstructed in modern consciousness, and an image is released!

The magnificent ruins of New Grange now appear before my eyes (see front cover). I see a mouth, from which emanates a collection of spirallic forms, directed perhaps to those gathered below, radiating outwards from the center, like a sector of a circle.

Now, from the listener's standpoint, I see a rising and tapering to a point, to the place where speech emanates from the high priest standing at the mouth of the cave. Priest—the cave's mouthpiece, inspired to speak the cave's spirallic wisdom out to the people waiting below!

New Grange, magnificent ruin of a long-gone culture, now lies mute, as its former mystery is appropriated to the needs of a growing tourist industry. But the *real* New Grange still lives, yes, still "out there" in the real world, *as* the real world—its very Being. It too lies mute. It needs its modern priests, its mouthpieces, in order to speak. It speaks in spirals, vortices. What would such speech *sound* like, and where would it's meaning *take* us if we spoke its turnings as they coil around us?

What would it *say*, in saying through *us*, its mouthpieces?

R ENAISSANCE

I feel we're in a very shabby moment, and neither the literary nor the musical experience really has its finger on the pulse of our crisis. From my point of view, we're in the midst of a flood of biblical proportions. It's both exterior and interior. At this point it's more devastating on the interior level, but it's leaking into the real world. I see everybody holding on in their individual way to an orange crate, to a piece of wood, and we are passing each other in this swollen river that has pretty well taken down all the landmarks, and pretty well overturned everything we've got.

(Leonard Cohen)

The "leakage" from the interior into the exterior world is a poetic way of saying that a breakdown is occurring in the centuries-long habit of thought that we could call the inner/outer disjunction. I have explored this breakdown for thirty years under various names, particularly that of the "end of the world" by which I mean the end of a habitual structure of thought that gives rise to stable appearances. This essay expands a new thought that came to me in a dream. It said simply: It's about a renaissance!

A Dream at Year's End

> A man is lying down, depressed. Another has whispered in his ear and I wonder if the depressed man is poisoned by the speech but I ask him, what did this other say to you. He tells me that the other whispered, "It's about a renaissance!" at which point his depression transforms into joy.

A renaissance! This revelation came at a time of bleakness in my own thought, as 2015 came to an end. I had recently completed my 13th book, and thirty years of concentrated research on the meaning of the "end of the world" suddenly came to a close. I was done! Nothing more to say! That final book had accomplished it and I was that very accomplishment. What the book said had come home to roost. I was now living those words. For thirty years I had been pulled in two directions, felt to be drastically opposed to each other, and almost torn in two.

The vertical direction opened me up to what I called the reality of living thinking or visionary experience. I danced there for years with the angels and was confronted by the demons. It was intoxicating, it was terrifying, and I eagerly sought its gold. I was simultaneously drawn into the horizontal domain of what I can now call the living body: earthly or ordinary reality, yes, but not quite the same as the empirical reality of science with its subject-object disjunctive consciousness.

The visions I received over the years were thus received in the living body, with the result that I heated up like a lamp, and remained in this fiery state for decades. I was somehow to live the incarnation of living thinking, since that was the process that "wanted" to happen. I had no idea how to do that but, since I could not do otherwise, I had to find a way of going about my ordinary life while being blasted by "fire."[1]

With the completion of my last book the fires were cooled at last. Thirty years of a sustained ordeal, along with my efforts to understand it, drew to a close. I fell into a dark depression. My dreams began to show movement of loss, finality, and inevitability. There was no "going back" to what was familiar:

> I am faced with my worst feelings, worst mood of being trapped, no resources, no escape. Living with my mother who has the face of malice. Getting a job at a Catholic school as a teacher, a live-in arrangement. I know nobody, I am ignored, not told what to do, where to be. I wander about, lost, aimless. The feeling darkens to a nightmarish congealing of despair. I even wake up out of it but sense the importance of staying in it. So I choose to re-enter the dream. It is there, waiting. Now I am approached by a dwarf! He is the one in power now. He asks if I want to join him in an activity. Totally unexpected, an invitation to play! This moment initiates a turn. Slowly the mood begins to change, lighten, I meet and greet more students, even begin to teach a little, spontaneously, out of the moment as they stand there, chatting. No formal teaching, just in the midst of a conversation, or as part of that conversation. I also realize that these students have a love of learning, a surprise. The whole mood changes, an enantiodromia! The same world takes on a

different face. I need a new word for what
happens in that conversation.

The Visionaries: AE, PETRARCH, JUNG

Within that dream conversation, a conversion
happens, from despair to joy, just as it did in my
"renaissance" dream. There is some potent connection
between this kind of transformation, be it an
enantiodromia or not, and what my dream named as a
renaissance. I felt a gathering enthusiasm for probing this
question more deeply and, as it happened, I had just been
re-reading a book by an Irish master-poet and visionary,
AE.2 His chapter Slave of the Lamp seems to be
describing a similar movement in his soul life. He tells
several experiences that, together, open him up to a new
reality.

At the conclusion of the previous chapter, The Earth
Breath, AE tells us about his black depression,
occasioned by the disparity between the visionary state
and ordinary reality:

> [T]he very intensity of vision made the recoil
> more unendurable. It was an agony of darkness
> and oblivion, wherein I seemed like those who in
> nightmare are buried in caverns so deep beneath
> the roots of the world that there is no hope of
> escape ... in those black hours the universe, a
> gigantic presence, seemed at war with me.

From within this despair, AE became aware of a
"swift echo or response to my own moods in
circumstance which had seemed hitherto immutable in its
indifference." Uncanny "affinities" between his inner
state and the things of the world began to appear:

"I have glanced in passing at a book left open by someone in a library, and the words first seen thrilled me for they confirmed a knowledge lately attained in vision."3 He goes on to describe many such adventures, culminating in an exultant realization of a new reality, one that he had previously not known about. AE was transported from a world in which one has no power over circumstance, to a living universe, flowing with "meaning and law." The discovery of this world transformed his depression into joy.

AE had discovered an uncanny affinity between his inner state and certain outer appearances that were attracted to him, and, in turn, I found my discovery of his text and its affinity to my dreams equally uncanny and exciting. But there was more to come. My dream spoke of "a renaissance", so I pulled down a book from my shelf, one that I had not read much at all. It is called "Life of Petrarch."

Petrarch is credited with inaugurating the Italian Renaissance and there is an identifiable moment in his life when the Renaissance can be said to be born in him —a moment in which an outer appearance coincided with an inner readiness to hear a "message." He was climbing Mt. Ventoux at the age of 32, with his brother.

Already deep in meditation, he was sensing the allegorical or soul meaning of his ascent when, arriving at the summit and surveying the grand view displayed before him, he opened a random page of the small copy he had of Augustine's Confessions and read (Book X, Ch. 8):

> Men go forth to marvel at the mountain heights,
> at huge waves in the sea, at the broad expanse of
> flowing rivers, at the wide reaches of the ocean,
> and at the circuits of the stars, but themselves
> they pass by.

The coincidence between this text and Petrarch's pressing inner concerns (his lack of spiritual progress) stunned him and constituted what has been called his conversion to a new spiritual path, inaugurating at the same time what we now call the Italian Renaissance. Although there is controversy regarding Petrarch's account (a letter that may be fictional in character, i.e. a rhetorical device, or a reference to something he actually did), there can be no doubt that a real conversion or awakening to a new kind of reality took place in Petrarch. Some years later, he wrote Secretum (The Secret) which continues and develops his dialogue with "Augustine". This book gives us a glimpse of the reality that Petrarch gained access to, or was initiated into through his dialogue with Augustine.[4]

Petrarch, like AE, suffered from depression (accidie) and his three dialogues with Augustine are a record of his conversion out of depression into his vocation as a man of letters, a poet, and the father of Humanism, "with one foot on earth and the other in heaven." He conceived of his conversion in terms of a kind of surgery, from the physician Augustine, who says:

> I have not at all as yet touched upon the deep-
> seated wounds which are within, and I rather
> dread the task when I remember what debate and
> murmuring were caused by even the lightest
> allusion to them. But, on the other hand, I am

not without hope that when you have rallied your
strength, your spirit will more firmly bear without
flinching a severer handling of the trouble.[5]

Petrarch replies, "have no fear on that score. By this
time I am used to hearing the name of my maladies and
to bearing the touch of the surgeon's hand." Augustine
diagnoses Petrarch's illness as being vexed with Fortune.
By this he means that Petrarch so far only knows a reality
of happenstance, one in which he has no "power over
circumstance", just as AE thought. Augustine seeks to
elevate Petrarch out of misery through a ruthless
methodology of negating the things of the world,
principally through a meditation on death and contempt
for earthly things. Petrarch also has to learn to think
differently and Augustine shows him how: "the words I
would have you say are these: instead of saying you
cannot, you ought to say I will not". In thinking, "I will
not" instead of "I cannot",

Petrarch is being initiated into the same reality that AE
found, some centuries later, a reality saturated with
meaning, in which appearances are attracted to him,
"related by affinity to some yet unrealized forces in my
being."[6] The dialogue between Augustine and Petrarch
places Petrarch in a tension (one foot on earth and the
other in heaven). He could not fully accede to
Augustine's admonition to abandon all his attachments to
the things of the world, although he agreed with much
of what his mentor said. This tension seems to have
broken open a world hitherto unknown.

Petrarch gives us a clear vision of this new world
when he reads a passage from Virgil, "There, in a cave

profound, King Æolus Holds in the tempests and the noisy wind, Which there he prisons fast. Those angry thralls Rage at their barrier, and the mountain side Roars with their dreadful noise, but he on top Sits high enthroned, his sceptre in his hand."

Petrarch now gives a unique interpretation of this passage:

> I have heard with my ears the fury, the rage, the roar of the winds; I have heard the trembling of the mountain and the din. Notice how well it all applies to the tempest of anger. And, on the other hand, I have heard the King, sitting on his high place, his sceptre grasped in his hand, subduing, binding in chains, and imprisoning those rebel blasts, who can doubt that with equal appropriateness this applies to the Reason? However, lest any one should miss the truth that all this refers to the soul and the wrath that vexes it, you see he adds the line and calms their passion and allays their wrath."

James Hillman's pioneering interpretation of the Italian Renaissance claims that, "it is not the return from nature to man that starts the Renaissance going, but the return to soul."[7] Based on my reading of Secretum, I would have to disagree in part with this assessment. There was no return to soul taking place but rather, a discovery of a hitherto unknown locus of soul, i.e., within language. Petrarch inaugurated an entirely new reality, one in which language was now felt to be alive, filled with meaning, and self-referential. Although future readers may have understood Petrarch's interpretation of Virgil as pointing to inner states of human beings (their emotions, reason, etc. i.e., Humanism), the passage above suggests strongly to me that Petrarch was awakened, through the tension that his dialogue with Augustine the physician heightened in him, to the reality of the world of literature in which soul or psyche is now reflecting itself. Petrarch needed Augustine's unsparing physician's hand to detach Petrarch from "natural" appearances (the things) but not from earthly attachments altogether. Instead, a new living universe opened up for Petrarch. We can see further evidence of this living universe in the way Laura, a real woman whom Petrarch loved, transformed into a living literary figure for his entire life; or, we could point to Secretum, and his dialogue with the living figure of speech that went by the name of Augustine. Petrarch also wrote letters to past historical figures and literary masters. They were alive for him!

In a word, Petrarch and AE were initiated into the reality of what we call today fiction, or the living world of literature. They were concerned with the truth of the imagination, as reflected in language. Both underwent an initiatory process, beginning with depression and ending in joy, just as my dream shows. Like Petrarch, AE discovered a "new earth" which he calls the "Many-Coloured Earth"—an earth that the "ancient seers worshiped as Deity," in which "live a divine folk ... temples wherein the gods do truly dwell ..." AE is clear that he is not referring to what we would now call empirical reality. He opens up to the Many-Coloured Earth "with the eyes of the body shut as in sleep," where he could see "valleys and hills, lustrous as a jewel ... when I came back to myself my own world (i.e. empirical reality—my insert) seemed grey and devoid of light though the summer sun was hot upon the sands."[8]

In this way AE is an eloquent modern spokesman for the literary reality that Petrarch inaugurated in early 14th century.

My dream shows an analogous kind of initiation (from misery to happiness, as Dante's Comedy also shows) but is it an awakening into the same reality as that of Petrarch and AE? If my dream had said, "It's about the Renaissance," I might be inclined to think so, but my dream says it is about a renaissance," a very different matter altogether. And the transformation from misery to joy occurs in the very speaking of those words. But how does this work? How does speaking the words that are annunciated to the depressed man initiate him into, and at the same time, constitute a new reality? And how is this reality different from the discoveries of AE and Petrarch? Finally what difference does it make that this transformation occurs in a dream, and not in waking life, as occurred to Petrarch and AE?

For Petrarch, a dialogue took place that was purely fictional and at the same time, transformative and constitutive. His encounter with Augustine placed him in a tension between the life of the spirit and the claims of the earthly realm of desires. This tension broke open the realm of living language or literature in which desire (e.g. his desire and love for "Laura" and a host of other literary figures) could find a new home. Petrarch discovered the reality of the psyche as reflected in language. Literature became the new mirror in which soul life could reflect itself. The death that Petrarch underwent at the hands of his physician of the soul, Augustine, was the death of his attachment to a world in which Fortuna ruled, where "penury, grief, disgrace, illness, death, and other evils too that are reckoned among the greatest, often befall us in spite of ourselves, and never with our own consent". Augustine strived throughout the dialogues to bring Petrarch out that world of contingency, through meditations on death, into a world in which what ever happens is willed: "Our conditions were to lay aside all juggling with terms and to seek truth in all plain simplicity, and the words I would have you use are these: instead of saying you cannot, you ought to say you will not."

AE found his way into this world too: "I knew that all I met was part of myself and that what I could not comprehend was related by affinity to some yet unrealized forces in my being" (i.e., willed). The world that Petrarch inaugurated and AE re-discovered is one in which appearances emerge spontaneously and autonomously, yet, and this is crucial, these figures are willed all along. In this world of living language, we have to learn to think "willed spontaneity"!

We can better understand this thought in terms of modern dreaming. Although the dream ego can be subjected to all sorts of penury, grief, illness, etc. there is also a way in which the psyche arranges or authors the whole thing. As Wolfgang Giegerich says, in relation to Jung's confrontation with the unconscious, a confrontation that, like Petrarch and AE, initiated him into a new reality[9]:

[I]t is my opinion that we must not take the surging tide of emotions and images, i.e., the incidence of the crisis, simply for granted as a given fact. Much rather, the critical situation itself must already be viewed psychologically: not as fate, an "objective necessity," but so to speak as "artificially" posited and staged by the soul solely on the basis of *its* own necessities. Viewed in this way, namely as a purposive arrangement, a literally "functional" disorder brought on for a very particular purpose … . a *psychological* crisis, by no means caused by nonpsychological empirical conditions originating in his personality or biography (e.g., constitutional factors, vicissitudes in early childhood, his having been conditioned by a certain adverse family constellation), but brought about solely by or rather *for* soul purposes, logical purposes.

This new reality that Petrarch inaugurated, as we can see, has a complex phenomenology. It can only be "found" through a death experience (depression, accidie …) that negates natural phenomena or appearances as no longer carrying "soul". Apparently, at the time of Petrarch, the sensible world was already no longer saturated with meaning, available to "speak", and to make claims on us, guiding, and shaping our existence. It was a world of happenstance. Even though Petrarch called it a world ruled by Fortuna, he could not experience any "divine will" at work in it. "Fortuna" seems only to be a worn-out trope for the accidents of a contingent life. His dialogue with Augustine initiated him into a new world, the world of literature with its living figures of speech whose appearances have the complex phenomenology of being, at the same time, willed and spontaneous. For example, Secretum is a dialogue in which Petrarch is constantly surprised, often unpleasantly so, by "Augustine's" challenges to his "world view," yet the entirety of the book is "arranged" by Petrarch for the purpose of displaying or bringing into manifestation a new reality—language as the carrier of psychic reality, a reality that has its own purposes and thus "arranges" appearances that are often a total shock to the ego.[10] Both AE and C. G. Jung were initiated into this "literary reality" in a very similar process to that of Petrarch. For example, in Jung's Liber Novus, Jung presents himself, as Petrarch did in Secretum, as constantly being surprised with unexpected responses from the "other". But as Giegerich notes:[11]

> It is the "superficial observer" and fantasy-syntonic I in the Red Book that says, "It has happened thus to me. And it happened in a way that I neither expected nor wished for". In truth, however, there is from the outset a powerful will or craving underlying it all, which shows itself time and again in the Red Book.

These three visionaries are showing us that this new reality is one that surrounds us, has its own intentions or will, and can make a ontological claim on us, drawing us into participation with its telos, appearing in unexpected, even shocking ways to the ordinary consciousness of the human participant. At the same time, this "other" cannot be thought of as being a separate entity. It is also in some crucial sense, us, and its locus is language, which now can be experienced as alive, as such, or as Petrarch discovered, the living world of literature. We can get a sense of the aliveness of this world when we hear for example, that Jung would spend hours strolling in his garden at Zurich, conversing with Philemon, a purely literary figure of speech.[12]

Renaissance

Returning to my renaissance dream with this historical backstory in place, it seems from the outset that, although the initiation process in the dream bears a remarkable analogy to that of Petrarch, AE, and indeed Jung, the phenomenology of *this* renaissance is quite different. Thee are three levels of "reality" to consider, for example: the whispering one speaking in the ear of the depressed one, who then speaks or manifests what he has heard and who undergoes the transformation, and the one who can perceive both levels (visionary and ordinary) simultaneously, all within the dream. A renaissance is announced and perhaps "performed" as this complex logical structure within *dream* reality.

Petrarch, AE, and Jung "heard" inner voices, such as "Augustine," or, as in case of AE, something that whispered to him, "Call it the Birth of Aeon!" or, as for Jung, "Philemon"—all talking in the waking state. They each then "spoke" the voice further into materiality, i.e. *literary* materiality. The whole process of receiving a voice and speaking it into materiality now occurs at the *dream* level of reality, not in a waking state, or what we call empirical reality today. But how are we to understand this?

For Petrarch and AE, a world had to be negated (world of Fortuna, world of immutability) in order for the new (literary) reality to emerge. Jung's transformation into a new reality is more complicated, and less understood by subsequent scholarship. He did not, as Hillman claims, merely discover imaginal reality, the living world of literary images—this was Petrarch's breakthrough. Jung himself was not ever able adequately to conceptualize the new reality he was initiated into.

Whereas Petrarch and AE found their way to a reality (call it fictional reality or Hillman's imaginal reality) that is quite distinguishable from ordinary reality (of circumstance, of the senses etc.—call it empirical reality today), Jung participated in a subsequent *union* of fictional reality and empirical reality—a form of consciousness for which we yet have no name. In this transformation, the habitual separation between fictional reality and empirical reality is negated. Or, we could say that the centuries-long separation between inner and outer is now abolished, yielding a form of literature (and corresponding consciousness) that is passing strange, and hardly noticed by subsequent scholarship.[13]

The possibility that the psyche is no longer interested in the inner-outer separation receives philosophical support from no less than Nietzsche (as read by Paul de Man in the following discussion) who challenged the most certain of axioms of empirical reality—the law of contradiction! As long as this law was said to refer to actual entities, we continuously affirm the existence of an outer, stable reality comprising "substance, self-identity, attribute, object, subject, action, etc." But Nietzsche has shown us that, rather than *reflecting* reality, the law of contradiction functions as a linguistic imperative, in effect *positing* such an apparent world (i.e. a world of appearances) that we have come to accept as the only one: "our belief in things is the precondition of our belief in logic ... [which] is, like the atom, a reconstruction of the "thing" ... Since we do not grasp this, but make of logic a criterion of true being, we are on the way to positing ... a metaphysical world, that is, a "true world" (—this, however, is the apparent world once more ...)."[14]

Nietzsche shows that, for millennia we have linguistically *posited* a firm and stable perspective that we call external reality, with its truth. It is not absolute but an *apparent* world—merely one way in which the world may appear, and a way that we have privileged because of the stability it brings, a world of permanent things that are logically independent of one another.

We can say that the psyche at one point "arranged" this development—that an external, stable reality was intended by psyche so that it could know itself as an external object, resulting at the same time in the flowering of a form of knowledge that rests on the subject-object disjunction (or inner-outer disjunction).

But the psyche is not beholden to us to continue in this way, and Jung's record of The Red Book shows in a quite startling way that the psyche may well be no longer interested in the disjunction at all, or for that matter, in supporting the law of contradiction and the apparent world that it posits.

What *new* apparent world could be emerging from a collapse of the inner-outer disjunction? I rather suspect that the renaissance spoken in my dream has something to do with this mystery. Let's be clear from the outset what consequences would follow if this were true. Almost every "fact" that we take for granted of our traditional (true) metaphysical world would be called into question: identity, substance, attribute, object, subject, action, cause and effect, selfhood, truth, knowledge—all these hypostases would collapse, a true end of the world phenomenon!

Further evidence of this collapse lies within the field of literary criticism where semiology (with its grammar/rhetoric distinction) teaches us the impossibility at times to decide whether a text has a literal (i.e. external reference) or a figural meaning (inner or literary meaning): "Rhetoric radically suspends logic and opens up vertiginous possibilities of referential aberration."[15]

We can approach the nature of the renaissance suggested in my dream by comparing the dream with say, the not-unusual situation in which a visionary (in the domain of external or outer reality) "hears" an inner voice and then "speaks" that voice into external reality through some art form. The crucial difference lies in the fact that both "external reality" (the depressed man) and "inner reality" (the voice which is then articulated by the depressed man) occur *within* the dream and there is a perspective that can perceive both as *within*. Whereas Petrarch was opened up to the reality of the "inner" or psychic life, as reflected in literature, this dream shows the psyche (interiority, inwardness) itself, i.e. *as such*, is undergoing a renaissance in which the inner/outer disjunction is now subsumed under interiority itself (the within-ness of the dream itself. What matters to psyche now, what is in the process of being born, is consciousness of interiority itself, and consciousness of the *psychic nature of the inner/outer disjunction* (i.e. it's all "inwardness"), rather than a literalization of externality or inwardness, which has driven our way of being and epistemology for millennia.

This new renaissance is the birth of consciousness of interiority or of the medium of the psyche *as such*! My dream shows that there is the perspective of the "depressed man" (ordinary reality); there is the perspective of the "other side" (visionary reality); and there is the new perspective that can embrace both realities. In general, this perspective is able to "perceive" the movements of psyche as it undergoes its transformations. This properly could be called psychic consciousness. It is a form of consciousness that does not identify with any particular perspective or content within the psyche but perceives the movements of psyche itself as it gives rise to various perspectives as "immanent relations" (self/self-as-other relations).

Jung did not achieve this level during his confrontation with the unconscious. He identified with only one element in his inner experiences, the fantasy-syntonic Jung, for whom each encounter was filled with immediacy, spontaneity, autonomy of the other etc. He was unable to take the perspective of psychic consciousness which would have shown the "willed arrangement" of the visions throughout Liber Novus, in the sense that Adler speaks, and in the sense that Jung later well understood in relation to hysteria and the neuroses.[16] He would have seen instead that the psyche, in its creative capacity, was creating, for the first time a new reality in which fictional reality and empirical reality are united, giving rise to an empirical manifestation of fictional reality.[17]

The New Appearances

I had a dream that gave the first hint of this renaissance thirty years ago. It was also a dream that gave me an insight into the later Jung's profound grasp of psychic reality as such.

> I am in our home then I am outside, by the side of the house. It is dark. E. comes. She is argumentative. She wants to know if I have sorted out my relationship with her, am I still involved, thinking of her etc. I am defensive at first, mumbling about discerning inner from outer reality but as I look at her I see with utter conviction that she is still involved with me, deeply and really wants to know that I am still as well, with her. Our relationship is real, our feelings for each other, the mystery. I blurt out that I am not interested in sorting out inner from outer , whether I projected anima onto her or whether I am to understand our relationship on an inner level refusing the outer reality etc. As I speak our desire grows and a kind of magnetic field begins to form in the darkness, vibrations of great energy begin to pulsate in the air. E. is afraid, tries to run but runs right into my arms. We embrace. We/I shout Look! Look! We see something emerging out of the darkness, a star, a speck of light moving about close, far, I don't know. I am getting filled with an immense power,

as this tiny light seems to approach. It is moving
about as if looking for a place to lodge. Did it
lodge in us? Awe fills me. I feel love, awe, and
being filled to bursting. I wake up with this
feeling. It is early Christmas Eve.

This dream, so long ago now, heralds the birth of a
new (psychic) consciousness, one that depends on the
"collapse" of the inner/outer disjunction. This
renaissance is indeed a birth, emerging as consciousness
of the medium that surrounds, fills, and supports us—
the psyche. [18]

Nietzsche shows us that the metaphysical world of
things, separate and self-identical, each thing standing out
clearly in space and time, is only an appearance, as
linguistically posited and maintained through habits of
thought. How would the world appear to a consciousness
that apperceives the mind that creates *all* such
appearances in the first place?[19] This is a question of
finding the art forms that can convey this self-
consciousness from within the appearances, whatever
they may be in language, image, life ...

Since my chosen art form is writing, I can say a little
about my efforts in this direction. I have written thirteen
books now, the first being my doctoral thesis. At first I
was startled by the way they were all getting composed
but I could write no other way. It was a kind of "willed
surrender" as described by one colleague this way[20]:

The reader is taken into the experiences of the
author through a form of literature that may not
have a name at this point in time. It is a form of
writing that flowed spontaneously from the

author's hand ... The process involves memories of a kind of dual consciousness, interweaving of past present and future, inner and outer reality, along with philosophical thoughts expressed in direct speech which came to the author quite spontaneously. All these elements are brought to life in the adventures of the purely literary figures, David and Master John while the narrator is John, the author. Each character leads a separate life but are they really separate? The reader will discover the truth at the very end.

In writing my books I simply follow the productions of the psyche as they appear to me. A flow begins and although I am quite clear that I am writing, I also feel "something else" writing itself out though my hand, something I knew about all along although, as I said, it also comes as a total surprise.[21] In writing this way there is a "sudden discorporating slippage" that takes place, as Philip K. Dick says, a slippage in boundaries, solidity, separateness—an "end of the world" phenomenon, i.e. a metaphysical world and its logic of separation!

I have also begun to practice a style of discourse with others, in which I surrender any effort to separate inner from outer, memory from confabulation, etc., and instead try to hear the conversation simply as a story flowing from one to the other.[22] I have discovered that the self-identity of the isolated subject tends to soften and even disappear ... leaving what—simply the conversation, which begins to take on a life of its own—its own author. A clue to what may happen next lies in my dream of thirty years ago, "I blurt out that I am not interested in sorting out inner from outer, ... As I speak our desire grows and a kind of magnetic field begins to form in the darkness, vibrations of great energy begin to pulsate in the air. ... We see something emerging out of the darkness, a star, a speck of light moving about close, far, I don't know. I am getting filled with an immense power, as this tiny light seems to approach. It is moving about as if looking for a place to lodge. Did it lodge in us? Awe fills me. I feel love, awe, and being filled to bursting ... " This dream suggests strongly that "something else" may emerge into presence when established habitual categories of experience are broken down in a "catastrophe".

This presence may be a "renaissance"—a rebirth—of something "ancient," even primordial perhaps, and at the same time, giving impetus to and flowering of an entirely new way of being, and new definition of human beings.

---

[1] For my account of those years, see The Imperative and Mouthpiece, available at Amazon.

[2] AE: The Candle of Vision. University Books, London. 1965. 13.

[3] Ibid. 15-16.

[4] Quotes drawn from Petrarch's Familiar Letters and Secretum.

[5] At the same time of my "renaissance" dream I also dream of the physician of the soul: "I dream of a centaur, Chiron, healing by penetrating bodies with his right hand. At first there is an expression of horror in the face of the patient, but this transforms to one of joy." "Chiron" means "hand" and the root of "Chiron" is *gheb*, which gives rise to another word, surgeon!

[6] AE. Op. Cit. 17.

[7] Hillman, J: Revisioning Psychology. Harper, New York. 1992. 196-8.

[8] Op. Cit. Ch. Many-Coloured Land.

[9] Giegerich, W. The Soul Always Thinks. Spring Journal books, New Orleans. 2010, 182.

[10] The term, "arrangement" comes from Alfred Adler, "with great avidity, directly or by detours, … through the arrangement of symptoms, the neurotic strives for increased possession, power, and influence, …" Ansbacher, H. L. & R. R. The Individual Psychology of Alfred Adler. Harper, New York. 1956. 112.

[11] Giegerich, W. Liber Novus: That is, the New Bible. Spring Journal, Vol. 83. 2010. 373.

[12] Jung, C. G. Memories, Dreams, Reflections. Ch. Confrontation with the Unconscious.

[13] See my essay: The Hidden Legacy of The Red Book at https:// independent.academia.edu/WoodcockJohn

[14] de Man, P. Allegories of Reading. Yale University Press, London. 1979. 120.

[15] Op. Cit. 10.

[16] Not willed by Jung's ego anymore than Petrarch or AE felt they "willed" misery in their lives; rather, willed by a deeper more comprehensive subject that, as we will see, has an "end" in mind that Jung's ego knew nothing about.

[17] See my book, Oblivion of Being, and its Afterword for a more comprehensive exploration of this phenomenon. Available at Amazon.

[18] "The inner essence, the mind (mindedness) that fills, animates, guides me, and that … also "carries" or "supports" me"—Wolfgang Giegerich: The Soul Always Thinks. Op. Cit. 181.

[19] It's more accurate to ask what would the psyche perceive in its attainment as self-consciousness itself.

---

[20] See my book, Mouthpiece. Available at Amazon.

[21] See my latest book, The Peril in Thinking, for an excerpt from my doctoral thesis which displays this art form. Available at Amazon.

[22] See my book, Oblivion of Being, for a fictional account of this methodology. Available at Amazon.

RENAISSANCE, AGAIN

I ended my earlier essay, Renaissance, with these words: "I have also begun to practice a style of discourse with others, in which I surrender any effort to separate inner from outer, memory from confabulation, etc., and instead try to hear the conversation simply as a story ..."

A clue to what may happen next lies in my dream of thirty years ago (see above), "I blurt out that I am not interested in sorting out inner from outer. ..."

This dream suggests strongly that "something else" may emerge into presence when established habitual categories of experience are broken down in a "catastrophe".

This presence may be a "renaissance"—a rebirth —of something "ancient," even primordial perhaps, and at the same time, giving impetus to and flowering of an entirely new way of being, and new definition of human beings.

You can imagine my surprise at the "next thing" that happened: Another dream in which *she* appears to me again—and she has something to say.

Read on:

I dream:

> I am at a university, wandering around. I am at a rocky beach with a young lovely woman who seems very keen on me. I point out the violence of the chaotic waves to her, and, as I get increasingly interested in her, I ask, "What are you doing at this university?" She tells me, "I am sentenced here." "By whom, I ask?" "By a myth," she replies. A mood of erotic love pervades. At one point she climbs into my bed.

SHE: I am sentenced here by a myth.

ME: But we are living in a time that is free of myth. We call it nihilism. And furthermore, if you can say the word "myth", that syntax should assure you that you are, in consciousness, outside or beyond the various worlds (myths to us) that people, or entire civilizations, were embedded in. While they were so embedded or contained, they could never use the word "myth". Instead it was, for them, Life, Truth, or the gods, or even God. When we were able to reflect on all such worlds and call them all myths, then we were, and still are, psychologically at least, outside of mythical structures of consciousness. Myths are now a *content* of consciousness, a complete reversal of former ontological structures.

She snuggled in closer and I could feel her breast pushing against my flank. She became thoughtful, just when I was sliding out of my mind into my senses. She gazed at the ceiling and spoke:

SHE: Yes I see what you mean. I can really understand that consciousness has undergone transformations and that the biggest, perhaps of all, is a transformation out of containment in the mind-soaked world into what you told me is nihilism.

How did she know these terms, 'mind-soaked,' 'transformation,' I grew suddenly alert. I think those terms, and have done so for years. How could she come by these terms? Again I was brought back to my senses by the alluring scent of her body heat which seemed to almost overpower me. She casually wound her ankle around mine like a snake. She was still speaking.

SHE: Nonetheless, Johnny (how does she know my name?), I am sentenced here by a myth.

I was getting very disinclined to disagree with her. "Let nature take its course," I whispered, as I breathed in the musky fragrance of her hair and sunk deeper into the mattress. " How can you be so sure?" I could scarcely get the words out. "I'm sure," she said self-assuredly. She smiled into my eyes I drank her in deeply. Her face filled my vision; her mouth became a Beatrician smile, as the rest of her body seemed to melt away. My heart swelled in love—love for this strange young woman who seemed to know me so well. Our bodies seemed to twine together easily, with familiarity, as if we belonged together. She also seemed to know my arguments, my "way of knowing", and I had an unnerving feeling that she could easily "outplay" me under the tree of knowledge. She seemed to want something else though. What was it? O that smile, that smile … I fell into a dream, while she lay beside me softly breathing into my ear, "I am sentenced here by a myth."

A snake-like sentence floated in front of me. It read, "I am sentenced here by a myth." I received a slight jolt. Is the sentence itself speaking here? Has the sentence been sentenced here by a myth? I had taken my lovely companion to be the subject of the sentence telling me about some form of punishment she had received. But supposing she was simply speaking the speech of the sentence itself, as a mouthpiece for the sentence?

I woke up with a start. She was gone. A faint scent lingered. My senses were alive with her presence, the intimacy of our entwining bodies. She was real all right, but, I paused, what is the nature of that reality we shared, o so briefly? And why was she sent to me?

Was she to deliver a message?

As the day progressed, I continued to muse on my remarkable, and lovely, figure of speech. Her smile, just before I fell asleep, so Beatrice-like, was surely to direct my desire past her to the more essential matter. A sentence is telling me something about its life, as a sentence. It seems to be telling me that its origins lie in a myth. Maybe the origin of all sentences lies in a myth. Maybe there is a kind of prison sentencing at work too. Is the originating myth a kind of prison guard as well, preventing a sentence from being anything else? Does this also mean that my sentence, maybe all sentences, wants to be free in some way? Is this sentence for the life of my sentence? Is my sentence due to be pardoned? Does it want my help to escape its imprisonment? Perhaps if I turn my attention to the origin of the sentence, to its originating myth, I might get a clue about its possible imprisonment, if that were the issue.

As it happened I had been drawn briefly into a controversy concerning origin myths recently. There is a story of our origins being produced right now, backed by the money of Bill Gates, and spearheaded by historian David Christian. This world story is to tell us about our origins, and, like all origin stories is to give us the best account of who we are. He says of this huge project: "We're taking the best evidence from physics and the best evidence from chemistry and biology, and we're weaving it together into a story ..." I met him at a party recently and soon we were engaging in an energetic, enthusiastic discussion about this world story he was developing. I began to notice a problem that I brought to his attention and you can see it in the quote above. He and the project are gathering the best evidence from the hard sciences ONLY, in order to construct THE story of where we all come from and who we are. That is, he is telling a story of the evolution of exteriors only (the kind of reality that science can measure and verify) and therefore of us as verifiable "things" having no interiority, while leaving out all those disciplines that have an equal grip on the modern mind, and which speak to the history or evolution of us as psychic beings or us as being inward or interior, or dare I say it, being ensouled, i.e., us not only as things that physics can measure, but as beings participating in BEING.

I am referring to disciplines such as the history of language, etymology, language and consciousness, depth psychology, various philosophies of Being, etc., phenomenology, hermeneutics, all of which spring from and speak to our inwardness (the psyche) and its nature as historical movement. In short, no evolution of interiority is included in the project at all.

There the project remains silent and yet purports to offer all of us a story we all can live within, and be taught who we are! The psyche's speech or stories about its own origins or about us as beings, or about our future is silenced once again, in favour of a story about the development of external reality only, this time on a grand scale, soon to be taught throughout the world as OUR origin story. Our children are to think of us only as things emerging from a non-living universe that indeed can produce only more THINGS that the hard sciences can measure and verify!

Even more disturbing to me is the presumption that we humans can concoct a myth of origins and then believe that we can proceed to live within what we have so concocted, from the outside, as it were. Origin myths are always given to a people. You find yourself born into cultural practices that demonstrate your origins to you, without any reflection at all. It's just taken for granted as truth. For example, the Elizabethan great chain of being was taken for granted at the time. Everyone proceeded in their daily lives according to the truth that each person participated in the essence of stars, minerals, animals, etc. and descended from Eden. Nobody in Elizabethan times studied the great chain of being as a myth! We could only study origin myths, as myths, when consciousness had emerged from containment in all myths, including origin myths, into exteriority.

Wait a minute! My sentence must therefore be "exterior" to myth too, if it can reflect on the fact that it has been sentenced by a myth. In short, my sentence is conscious of its own status as sentence and of being sentenced by a myth. My young lover must therefore be the consciousness of the sentence personified, i.e. its sensual, imaginative aspect—and its mouthpiece—and, furthermore, a way of engaging my senses, my imagination, my being, in the fullness of participation. Her presence pulled me into full, "sensual," even erotic, participation with the sentence and its utterance.

Could I then talk to my sentence more? Would she return to continue our lovemaking, or, if that were not possible, perhaps we could pursue our conversation? Can I listen to her voice as the voice of the conscious sentence, or as the mouthpiece of living language?

ME: I want ...

SHE: Don't say a word (at the sound of her voice I begin to fray at the edges again). Just listen. With your whole body, just listen.

I am on my back and she lies on top of me, so that we touch all the way down to our toes. She places her mouth close to my ear and whispers, so that I not only hear her words but feel her moist, warm breath caressing the fine hairs of my ear canal, going ever more deeply. She is entering me in the most intimate fashion possible.

SHE: I am sentenced here by a myth. You see, John, there is a sense in which I have now become free of my sentence, in the very act of speaking my sentence to you. I have become free, in a sense, of the way that I have been sentenced by a myth, which sentencing also goes on. Now I can reflect on my sentencing, with your help. I can now ask, what is it to be sentenced by a myth? And what is it for a sentence to be sentenced by a myth, in particular? Do different myths sentence in different ways?

ME: I have never thought these things before, but I find your questions intriguing.

I was now deep in a trance-like state, under the spell of her whispering voice and the slight weight of her body. I no longer knew who was speaking, who was responding.

ME: Could we ask how myths, or a myth, shapes language from the start and therefore how language might get structured, or sentenced within a particular myth's determination?

SHE: We could, lover ... keep going, deeper and deeper.

Her breath seemed to penetrate and light up my brain.

ME: Grammar is responsible for sentence construction, isn't it? Is grammar a myth? A sentence, you, my dear friend, are subject ... Noam Chomsky, I have got to take a look at Noam Chomsky.

I wake up, alone, hot, with a racing heart. I'll be back. We need more backstory ... The next day I return. I lie down on my bed and wait. Soon, she is there, sitting on the edge of my bed, poised, unhurried.

ME: Well, I took a look at Chomsky's work on grammar and it seems he and his mentor Harris developed what's called the transformational-generative grammar system which opens up an inquiry into surface and deep structures of language. (I struggled to think the relevant passages that struck me.) The deep structure yields all the possibilities of sentences.

Chomsky's model aims to show how all sentences, and their surface structure (simple and composite), are generated in English from transformations of what he calls the deep structure. It seems to me that he understands this deep structure as determinative in some way, as far as all sentences go. That's what got me interested because myth, too, is determinative of our thought structures. (I was getting excited now, eager to show my lovely young companion what I had discovered).

The Deep Structure of language is essentially generative of all possible sentences from a finite number of kernels, plus semantic rules of transformation. It's like a seedbed of partial thought forms that, if known, can generate all possible sentences and, by the way, it excludes many surface structures as being "ungrammatical" because they violate the "rules". (Did I sense her startle a bit here?)

Shall I go on? (She remained silent, so I took that as a cue to continue.)

I read an article giving an example of what an ungrammatical sentence would be, according to Chomsky. Here it is: Green ideas sleep furiously! This is said to be ungrammatical because it violates the rule of semantic compatibility. Now, I wasn't sure about the technical meaning of semantic compatibility so I took a look on the Net and found this intriguing quote by Kovacs: "semantic rules reflect the relations of reality; a certain degree of isomorphism obviously exists between the correlations of reality and the rule of semantic compatibility." So, "green ideas sleep furiously" is malformed because ideas, fury, and sleep are not related in reality.

Now she was getting quite disturbed and I thought I knew why.

ME: Yes, I know this theoretical move eliminates poetic sentences and literature, or any sentence that does not refer to outer reality. Chomsky has invented another way to express the age-old formulation of the relation between language and reality in terms of form and content—here, the form is the surface sentence and the content is the deep structure of the sentence that determines the sentence's grammatical (or ungrammatical) form.

SHE: I am sentenced here by a myth. I can't fly!

She began to weep and curled up on my bed where, for the first time I saw her wings, torn and faded. My heart nearly broke. I waited for her sobs to ebb into soft snuffles. She wiped her nose on my shirt and looked calmly into my eyes.

SHE: What else did you find?

I suddenly sensed that something was at stake in all of this. My diving into a backstory to her plight had a purpose that perhaps she knew about more than me but she needed my words to reach that purpose. I felt that, in a way, she was already at the end of our discussion and together we were reaching that same end. I went on.

ME: I've been reading the work of Paul de Man lately. He speaks of this long-standing relationship between language and reality in terms of form and content in its modern garb. The older polarities of inside and outside have been reversed. Internal meaning (content) has become outside reference and outer form has become intrinsic structure, "it matters little whether we call the inside the content or form, the outside the meaning or the appearance. The recurrent debate … stands under the aegis of an inside/outside metaphor that has never been seriously questioned."

SHE: I question it!

Her reaction was fierce and final. I knew now that we were getting close to ... what? I had to go on.

ME: But de Man also explains how French semiology has demonstrated that the perception of the *literary* dimensions of language is largely obscured if one submits uncritically to the authority of reference—a kind of linguistic awareness that has never ceased to be operative in poets and novelists. You see, my poor girl, there has been an oscillating debate for centuries about the relation between language and reality that fundamentally depends on an unquestioned, prior, inner/outer separation.

SHE: It's killing me!

Wails erupted and I could not hold back my tears either, but what on earth am I crying about? After a time, her grief subsided, and, as I waited, I began to question what has "never been seriously questioned." I began to muse out loud, while she once again rearranged her face on my shirtfront.

ME: The "inner/outer" separation! As that separation reified over the centuries, it has hardened into a fiction/empirical reality disjunction that has contracted language into being merely an instrument of communication of one speaker to a hearer, no longer having any life of its own. Furthermore, this communication only makes sense when it refers unambiguously to a verifiable piece of empirical reality. Is there a myth at the bottom of this inner/outer disjunction?

This sudden, inspired thought burst in on me and to my complete surprise, she kissed me full on my lips. This embrace was completely welcome and I did not want to ask what brought it on. I leaned in for more of this nectar but she pulled back a little. I controlled my panting and asked if she were all right. And did I notice a little color bleeding into the tips of her wings?

SHE: Here, there, subject, predicate, chains bind me, verbs have wings, no, verbs wing forth, yes.

Her wings were quite clearly now beginning to unfold their tired creases, as more color flowed into the dry veins, filling them with pulsing life. I felt I needed to speak a little more.

ME: There is a mythic pair that seems to have informed Western culture since Greek times—the Dionysus/ Apollo pair. Our entire history has been understood in terms of the fluctuating degree of manifestations of Dionysus who is seen as Life or Being, while his brother Apollo creates distance from the crushing burden of life through reflection, art, distance. "To experience oneself is something absolutely radical, abyssal, because it only happens in suffering and in joy," says Michel Henry, who adds, "Dionysus is a god of desire or of life crushed against itself, in its joy and suffering. And this is a god who is burdened with self in a pathos so heavy that in effect he wants to relieve himself of his self. At bottom, Dionysus is the one who creates Apollo in order to distance himself from his self."

Nietzsche used this myth to say something essential about language, along the lines of the opposition of appearances and being or, in linguistic terms, the relationship between figural and proper meaning (the reference of the metaphor in which meaning and being coincide). The meaning or reference (Dionysus) engenders the metaphor (Apollo) as the appearance of this meaning.

Embedded in this view of our history is a genealogy of language which assumes an original language of exteriority which then somehow creates an "inner" figurative language. In other words the mythic pair, Dionysus/Apollo embody an inner/outer opposition, with a clear valorization of the "outer" which somehow creates the "inner." Our modern theory of evolution, and philosophy of consciousness are merely the latest formulations of this dichotomy. It runs through all our discourses unchallenged.

SHE: I challenge it!

Her wings were now fully unfurled and rich weavings of intense, iridescent color rippled though their cobweb veins. She stretched and yawned as if coming awake for the first time—in how long?

ME: Yes, it's time isn't it?

SHE: My sentencing is over, my chains fall at my feet. You, my lover, (I caught my breath, taking in her beauty with a gasp), have freed me.

ME: In turn, I commit myself to you. I voluntarily bind myself to you while you fly free. Where will you go?

SHE: Don't you remember that poem you wrote so long ago my lover? (How can *she* remember my memories? I felt momentarily disoriented).

ME: Now that you say it, yes, I think I do, (and I went to my poetry book to find it). Yes, here it is.

SHE: Read it to me now (and she lay down beside me and once again I became intoxicated with her scent of love)...

AND SO YOU COME TO ME

and so you come to me
in a joyful celebration of reunion
i gaze at your naked body
you change from young woman
to a young man and back again
i burst out in a startled joyous cry
o you are androgynous

licking my face
you become all tongue
wet warm
filling my senses

i am the object of your desire

now as i lie fully aroused
you tell of a meteor falling
through the sky towards earth
i see it as you so tell me
seeing and telling merge into one

image and word as one

you tell me quite clearly
in my arousal
in the fullness of my passion

what profound mystery is this my sister?

is my passionate arousal
a necessary preparation
a kind of readiness

a bow strung tautly
pulled back further and further
the arrow of consciousness notched quickly

am i then to follow its unerring path
leaving the quivering bow behind
flying free in the blue sky
of ecstatic vision
where you live
where you speak
in the clear language of visionary forms?

meteor falling
towards the earth
burning red
leaving a trail of dark burning fire
arcing through the sky
this vision
your sacred speech
my star sister

i will remember

you have told me something sacred
left me in deep wonder

what kind of speech what words
form a fiery meteor arcing through the sky
with immense crackling power

i will do my work now
my beloved star sister
you have done yours
to prepare the vessel

from the taut quivering of the bow
to the unerring flight of the arrow
to the target

a new world may thus be entered
a world of vast distance
crackling furnaces of fire
tremendous forces
of sheer titanic creation

a world of your speech
your word
where you speak me into existence

SHE (sighing): You do remember!

ME: Yes, I do. And I remember my vow of commitment to
      you, in a love ritual, so long ago...

      LOVE RITUAL

      i entered your home last night
      you welcomed me at the door
      i knew what it meant
      it meant you would let me in
      and so i entered

      body burning with a soft glow
      heart a pulsing animal
      i took your hand
      led you to your very own couch
      placing my head on your knee
      just for a moment

      then i said
      fetch a bowl of water, and a towel

and you did

tenderly holding your foot
hands hungering
i began to wash your foot

my body singing music to you
washing and caressing
pouring water-myself onto your skin

running over your body
sighing back into the bowl

i drink from that bowl
where we are now mixed
libation to the new life
that will emerge in your body

T HE COMING GUEST: *fountain-mouth*

. . . we say that the Judgment is distant or near, that the Millennium approaches, that a day of certain political, moral, social reforms is at hand, and the like, when we mean, that, in the nature of things, one of the facts we contemplate is external and fugitive, and the other is permanent and connate with the soul. The things we now esteem fixed shall one by one, detach themselves, like ripe fruit, from our experience, and fall. The wind: shall blow them none knows whither. The landscape, the figures, Boston, London, are facts as fugitive as any institution past, or any wisp of mist or smoke, and so is society, and so is the world. The soul looketh steadily forwards, creating a world before her, leaving worlds behind her. She has no dates, nor rites, nor persons, nor specialties, nor men. The soul knows only the soul, the web of events is the flowing robe in which she is clothed.

Ralph Waldo Emerson

Introduction

In a discussion of a typical dream in which the panicked dreamer is being chased by wild dogs, Wolfgang Giegerich describes the uroboric (circular) logic of dreams:[1]

> Is it, perhaps, not as simple as it seems, namely, that being chased is the cause of the running away, but just as much the other way around, that the escape shown in the dream is the reason for the chase by the dogs? … The end of the dream, escape and getaway, is perhaps its true beginning, and the beginning of the dream, the pursuit, is perhaps merely a consequence, something that follows on the heels of the escape.

What we normally, i.e. in our every-day ordinary consciousness, see as a beginning "causing" an end is, according to a deeper soul-perspective, reversed so that the end "causes" the beginning! In this dream we can thus see that the dreamer's panicky flight equally "causes" the dogs to chase after her. Entering the logic of the dream, we can see that, since either (linear) sequence is possible, we cannot privilege any one sequence without destroying the totality of the dream. The logic of the dream is circular, or uroboric, and generates a necessity, a psychological necessity. As Hillman would put it, when the dogs chase the panicky dreamer she runs, and when the panicky dreamer runs, the dogs give chase. If the dreamer can learn to think the entirety of this logic, "feeling" its *necessity* (i.e., how each "part" of the dream belongs to the totality, including the part she plays as the panicky fleeing one, then the dream phenomenon is fulfilled and it simply "retires".[2]

All along, the dreamer had been unconsciously participating in the dream's logic, tangled up in identification with one aspect of the dream (the dream-I), running from life, avoiding scary situations or the life of the instincts, refusing to live fully, perhaps refusing to follow the dogs as psychopomp into a deeper understanding of her being and Being. Thus, prior to the dream's appearance, it's logic was already unfolding in actuality through the dreamer's unconscious actions, demeanor, physiognomy and habits of thought, prejudices, pathology, or even physical illness.[3] In other words, the actualization of the dream in reality is determined by both the dream's necessity and the various ways the dreamer is unconsciously identified with one aspect or another of the dream.

I will call this kind of participation in a dream's necessity, *unconscious participation,* which term of course invites the question of *conscious* participation. What could unfold into life through the actions of a dreamer who has succeeded in gaining access to the entirety of the dream's uroboric logic, i.e. who had learned to think the dream from all its perspectives, not that of only the dream ego? Such a dreamer would be free of entanglement in the dream. But free to do what? Here, Giegerich falls silent or perhaps he would concede that the dreamer now can get on with her personal life, having been enriched in her soul depths by her struggles. This stance springs from Giegerich's privileging the soul in its aspect of pure spirit, methodologically following the philosophical work of Hegel. His profession as psychologist is rooted in the conviction that the soul "wants" to simply fulfill its logic, each soul moment thinking itself out fully, with the conscious participation of the human participant, so that it may "appear" as pure thinking, in the mind of the human being (as psychologist). Then it retires, or withdraws, as I said, leaving the human free to participate in other soul moments, or not.

In writing about our freedom, once attained, Owen Barfield writes:[4]

> We shall [then] be free to turn either outward towards what we perceive or inward towards what we *are*. ... It will be in the former direction that we shall turn, as Goethe did, when our primary concern is to have to do with spirit through nature, And, by perceiving nature as expression [of spirit—my insert], to realize for ourselves that matter is after all spirit. It will be in the latter direction that we shall turn, as Hegel did, when our primary concern is to have to do with the human spirit.

Obviously this choice, done in freedom, can only occur when all unconscious identifications are released and the dreamer is free to "read" the dream in its entirety.

The difference in these possible directions, once we are free of entanglements in the unconscious life of the dream, is determined by whether we regard dreams as only generating a task of thinking or more than this, a task of art. By "art" I mean a cultural practice that in some way makes evident to the senses ("expresses" or "incarnates") the invisible life of the soul or spirit. In this way I am extending Barfield's meaning of "nature" to include art work, or cultural productions that also are manifestations of soul life in the world of the senses.

We can think of this choice, made in freedom, in terms of orientation to the past or to the unknown future. Until we are free of our metaphysical presuppositions (habits of thought), we must remain oriented only to past forms of "nature". The epistemology of metaphysics rests on the acceptance of always already formed, stable, solid appearances. These unquestioned appearances determine what counts as knowledge, and, as such, metaphysical knowledge is always knowledge of the "past" (the already formed appearances). We make decisions regarding the (posited) future on the basis of this stable way of knowing the past (trends, predictions, statistics, models, plans, goals, etc.)

But what happens when the permanence of the stable, solid appearances is brought into question by individual experiences that simply cannot be understood in terms of the knowledge system of metaphysics?[5] Think of that scene in the movie, "The Matrix" where Neo accepts Morpheus' invitation to question the solid permanence of his world. He took the pill and found the appearances melting into a state of fluidity.[6] We seem to be living in a time when the (logic of) appearances (is)/ are undergoing an epochal transformation. What counted as knowledge no longer counts, in terms of orienting us to a very uncertain and unknown future. We need another way, and that way, I hope to show, is the way of art.

The following dream presents this choice, not only in the life of one dreamer, but also in the life of an entire historical time, when that time is seen in its entirety as a dream, an image of an age—the age of solidity, or of the substantial things—the metaphysical world!

The Age of Christ

> Early morning in the city, few people around. Some trams sidle into their station, ready to start the day. I drive into a bay. I will follow them. They start off and as I follow the road gets more and more rocky and narrow. Stones become boulders and all my forward motion is impeded. I get anxious and fearful ... then in the city, the broken down part, I see huge cranes lowering a long horizontal piece of stone into place. It is an art work called the "Petrified Christ".

As the dreamer, I was deeply impressed by the dream's movement as progressive constriction, marked by a mood of increasing anxiety reflected as impeding stones getting bigger until, finally, reaching its culmination as complete immobility and petrification. When all progress forward is halted this way, an art work is lowered into view, a sculpted stone called the Petrified Christ, appearing in the "location" of a breakdown (the broken part of the city). According the uroboric logic of dreams, I could equally say that the lowering of the Petrified Christ art work into view, as the true beginning, "causes" the increasing petrification of all progress. Only when all progress is halted, with a mood of alarm or anxiety, can the art work be revealed. The solidity of stone as an anxiety-provoking impediment to progress is transformed, at its culmination, into art. Not just any art but "The Petrified Christ"!

At this point of writing, my imagination is inflamed with new thinking, fresh possibilities, showing that, as the dreamer, I may no longer be so entangled in the dream, identified with the dream-I, suffering with increasing anxiety, as I did for many years. Instead, I am released into resonant imaginative response to the *entirety* of the dream. Is the petrified Christ the image "informing" the linear progress of history over the last 2000 years of the Christian era—an era marked by reification of thought, along with its corresponding stable appearances in the world?[7]

Heidegger says the essence of the being of art is to open to a world: "By the opening of a world, all things gain their lingering and hastening, their distance and proximity, their breadth and their limits" [i.e., their belongingness].[8] Accordingly, The petrified Christ, as an *image*, reveals a past age and its characteristic notion of linear historical time, i.e., the Christian Age, in its entirety. But the Petrified Christ as an *art work* opens us up to a new world, and as such, is an inception.[9]

My dream shows that linear "motion", the past constrained to move forward towards a future end (the apocalypse), is the "Christian" understanding of temporality. The things appear as solid appearances (surface only, having no soul depth) that increasingly impede "progress", with a corresponding intensification of anxiety.[10]

There is an analogous account of progress leading to complete petrification followed by transformation into a new world. Dante's Comedy describes Dante, with his guide Virgil, and later, Beatrice, progressing from misery to happiness by way of descent into Inferno and then upwards to Purgatorio, and finally to Paradiso. As he descends through the levels of Hell, he travels a spirallic path that becomes more and more constricting and cold. He reaches the centre of the Earth and finds Satan, at the nadir of his descent. Satan is completely enclosed in ice, an image of petrification. He beats his mighty wings and this action only has the effect of fanning the icy winds and freezing him even more firmly—a colossal symbol of futility! What happens next is an astonishing act of the imagination. Dante the author somehow is able to picture what would happen, in terms of a reversal of gravitational pull, as the travellers reach the centre of the earth by clambering down the body of Satan from head to his "haunches" (the absolute centre of the earth). Virgil turns around and starts to climb *up* the leg of Satan towards his feet and then towards the surface of the opposite side of the earth, so that Satan's head is now felt to be below them. Gravity is now reversed:[11]

> I clipp'd him round the neck, for so he bade; And noting time and place, he, when the wings Enough were op'd, caught fast the shaggy sides, And down from pile to pile descending stepp'd Between the thick fell and the jagged ice. Soon as he reach'd the point, whereat the thigh Upon the swelling of the haunches turns, My leader there with pain and struggling hard Turn'd round his head, where his feet stood before, And grappled at the fell, as one who mounts, That into hell methought we turn'd again. "My guide! vouchsafe few words to set me free From error's thralldom.
>
> Where is now the ice? How standeth he in posture thus revers'd? And how from eve to

> morn in space so brief Hath the sun made his
> transit?" Thus answering spake: "Thou deemest
> thou art still On th' other side the centre, where I
> grasp'd Th' abhorred worm, that boreth through
> the world. Thou wast on th' other side, so long as
> I Descended; when I turn'd, thou didst o'erpass
> That point, to which from ev'ry part is dragg'd
> All heavy substance. Thou art now arriv'd Under
> the hemisphere opposed to that ...

When Dante "arrives" in Purgatory, he has not literally left Hell. In fact he has never gone anywhere at all. He is always in the same "place" as it undergoes its self-transformations. The appearances of Hell are taken to their logical limit of complete petrification and a transformation occurs where the appearances become those of Purgatorio, along with a transformed notion of temporality. Temporality in Inferno is "eternity" but in Purgatorio time is defined in terms of self-imposed efforts towards the purification of sin. There is a way out when the sinner is purified. Purgatorio is perhaps an "archetypal" model of therapeutic time. It ends when the sinner wills it to end.

The appearances alter according to the state of consciousness that accords with each of the three worlds. Dante needs his guides, Virgil, and later, Beatrice, to educate or initiate him into the consciousness of each new world he has entered. In order for the new appearances to *be*, consciousness must also transform.

Dante demonstrates this essential correspondence between consciousness and appearance in two ways: the topography of each world is similar: Inferno, Purgatorio, and Paradiso each have the same number of levels; Inferno and Purgatorio are spirallic but inverse topologies, etc. The language (consciousness) of each world is unique to that world and correlates to the way things appear in that world. For example, in Inferno, the language is that of subject-object and the things appear in their separateness. Bodies are scorched by fire, stabbed, flayed, chewed, etc. Dante is ordered by Virgil to keep moving, and not to interpenetrate with the consciousness of the damned (e.g. by empathizing with their suffering). To do so would have the consequence of getting caught in Hell. Dante was simply not prepared. In Paradiso on the other hand, the language is that of interpenetration, predominantly as transparent images of light:[12]

> It seemed to me that we were covered by a cloud/Shining and thick, as if polished,/Like a diamond which has been caught by the sun. ... / If I was body (and here we cannot conceive/ How one dimension can contain another/As must happen if bodies interpenetrate.)

Finally, Dante arrives at the pinnacle of his journey from misery to happiness: The White Rose. By analogy to my dream, the Rose is the supreme symbol of Dante's entire temporal journey through Hell, Purgatory, and Paradise. He discovers that the various permutations of will and desire, and their corresponding appearances in the three worlds, are all expressions of "the love that moves the sun and stars." In other words the same "place", Earth, appears *as* the worlds of Inferno, Purgatorio, and Paradiso, in accord with the correlative consciousness of each world. Dante's final vision of the

White Rose shows what happens when the entirety of the "journey" is beheld: All the appearances throughout the journey from misery to happiness, in their entirety, are subsumed under the singular vision of the White Rose. Dante's consciousness is simultaneously transformed to one in which "my will and desire were turned by love."[13] When consciousness reaches a state in which will and desire are united, the earth appears as a single many-petalled White Rose (every *thing* is an appearance of Love). This spiritual attainment is surely a Western version of attainment of Ajna consciousness by Kundalini masters who have reached the level where there is still just a small separation between self and the totality of everything else—pictured as two petals or wings.

Dante's poem shows that severity of sin is the constricting factor in Hell. Sin may be seen as separation from God and the greatest sinner, Satan, is completely immobilized in maximum separation from God. My dream shows rocks and boulders as the constricting power of progress, resulting finally in complete immobilization and anxiety. Instead of the theological language of sin, we can think of the language of reification. The etymological root of "reify" is *res*, meaning "thing". My dream, as amplified by an interpretation of Dante's Comedy, suggests there a connection between "progress" and the reification of things or appearances.

Heidegger teaches us that the essence of the scientific mind is its capacity to generate a world picture. Man becomes the subject and centre of reference of beings as such. The world is grasped as a picture, which means that a being (appearance) *is* only insofar as we can *represent* it in the world picture.[14] The natural world is logically overcome by our representations of that world. We achieve this "victory" by language of category, measurement, quantity, etc. This picture is reified through habitual use of language, for the sake of generating a stable world whose representative character is gradually forgotten, finally replacing the natural world altogether. We call this domination of the natural world through reifying language, progress.

The fact that our modern world is defined as the rapid explosion of technological innovation is not a counter-argument to my contention of petrification here. These innovations are things belonging to our world picture, not the natural world that in fact is becoming exhausted. The things of the natural world gain *being*, or appearance, in our world picture only as "natural resources", to be exploited for the sake of stabilizing the technological world (picture, but forgotten as such). In other words the speed with which technology is moving today only serves to further reify its status as "*the* world", its *representative* nature now being completely forgotten.

Solidification (reification) of the object occurs when we forget the representative nature of language and "take things literally". The object now "stands alone" losing its former character, as a representative of God's creation for example (nature could once be read as a sacred text):[15]

> By degrees we may come to know the primitive
> sense of the permanent objects of nature, so that

> the world shall be to us an open book, and every
> form significant of its hidden life and final cause.

Even though we may acknowledge the Internet, for example, as sheer movement now, we continue to read (interpret) this technological phenomenon, not as a sacred text, but as a literal thing, thereby deepening the petrification of the world in which this literal thing appears. Its "movement" is seen only as mechanical or digital movement (i.e. positivized). To read the Internet phenomenon as a "sacred text" would be to initiate another kind of movement altogether—a soul movement taking us more deeply into the unfamiliar, the unknown, the *otherness* that constitutes the Internet phenomenon in the first place (i.e., the formal cause). Clearly this kind of movement has disappeared from consciousness with the "death of God" and we are left ontologically in state of petrification.

Wolfgang Giegerich has shown us that, from the soul's point of view, the "historical" ontological foundation to the scientific mind is that of a momentous transformation in the soul, one that inaugurates the Christian Age, or linear historical time in the first place. As he says:[16]

> [L]inear historical time, the time in which the events of physics, the evolution of the species, the history of mankind, as well as our individual lives occur, is the product of an original invention and manufacturing. Of course, this manufacturing does not take place in factories, but in the primary industry of the soul's imagination.

My dream, then, seems to show the relationship between linear history, in its character of progressive movement, reification, and the image of the petrified Christ as an art form. Giegerich speaks further in his essay, of the Judeo-Christian Age in essence being an arrested or frozen moment of time since, as a soul moment, it cannot ever be fulfilled, and is always deferred to an apocalyptic future.[17] His analysis of the archetypal soul movement underlying our current technological civilization gives us an eye-opening account of the soul of modern everyday life:[18]

> [E]xistence in time becomes a waiting, an expectant looking for Him. The qualitative moment is no longer in itself rounded and complete. The expectant waiting is the psychological reflex of the retained breath, and also the reflex of the fixed, arrested truth (present), which as arrested is prevented from exhausting and completing itself. ... What the arrest does is to sunder the moment into its *arche* on the one hand and its *telos* on the other, and by distending them produce an immense internal tension corresponding to this nuclear fission. ... This is a tension that, at the end of the Christian eon when it has receded from an objective spiritual level into the personal life and the subjective empirical feelings of the individual, has to be constantly re-experienced and re-enacted by means of thrilling novels or movies. One needs pastimes and diversions to kill the empty time between the severed halves of the one present arrested in its course and to make the endless waiting for the systematically deferred

ending endurable.

The petrified Christ is a symbol of the petrification of *all* soul moments (commonly known as Paganism) into one moment of time that stretches linearly as progress towards an apocalyptic end. This interpretation gives us a way to understand the strange association of progress with petrification/reification and the image of Christ.

But now I am drawn to the question of art. Why does the dream present the image of the petrified Christ as an *art work*? Is it only to disclose the world of the Christian Age to us? Could there also possibly be an inception—a disclosure of a new world, one that may emerge with the fulfillment of the given world (picture) of our technological civilization?

> The history of the Christian West, as the history of the saved-up, arrested moment, had to run up to the apocalypse. The apocalypse, however, may now be conceived as the end of only this one moment, not as the end at large. As long as we fear the apocalyptic end of history through an atomic or environmental catastrophe as the absolute end, it is we who still equate this one moment of time with time at large, and thereby show to what extent we are blindly imprisoned in this single moment. The apocalypse, if it had occurred, would be the end of this imprisonment and the entrance into new moments, new presents.[19]

The Petrified Christ as a *work of art* is one unexpected detail that seems to me to show a transformation out of history-as-progress towards an apocalyptic end and into a new soul moment characterized by *art work*. This possible transformation needs some discussion, along the lines that Heidegger suggests, "are we, in our existence, historically at the origin? Or do we, rather, in our relationship with art, appeal, merely, to a cultured knowledge of the past?" There is a decision to be made! Heidegger recalls Hegel's famous conclusions concerning the nature of art:[20]

> Art no longer counts as the highest way in which truth finds existence for itself. ... One may well hope that art will continue to advance and perfect itself, but its form has ceased to be the highest need of spirit. ... In all these connections art is, and remains, with regard to its highest vocation, a thing of the past.

Rather than criticizing these conclusions, Heidegger seeks to locate them in the web of historic meaning that surrounds them: "Behind [Hegel's] judgment there stands Western thinking since the Greeks, a thinking which corresponds to a truth of beings that has already happened." There is a decision to be made re: Hegel's judgment, according to Heidegger, and it is a decision regarding the nature of truth. Heidegger has shown, in his essay, The Origin of the Work of Art, that art shows, or opens up as an inception, a truth that:

> [C]an never be verified or derived from what went before. In its exclusive reality, what went before is refuted by the work. What art founds, therefore, can never be compensated and made good in terms of what is present and available for use. *The founding is an overflowing, a bestowal.*[21] [my italics]

The founding character of art means that art does not

just have a history along with other things but that art is the ground of history. Art discloses a new world and its appearances, generating what will become a new history. If we believe that art only deals with the already-given appearances then we must agree with Hegel that art is now irrelevant to the truth of the already given things (since Hegel revealed and exhausted that truth of metaphysics in thought). My dream art work of the Petrified Christ could then only refer to, in an irrelevant way, the past Christian Age, and its fulfillment.[22] But keep in mind: to decide that way, i.e., Hegel's way, we would have to ignore or dismiss the anomaly in my dream, the Petrified Christ as an art work! To accept the anomaly, without a traditional interpretation, is to place us, along with Heidegger, in a relationship to art as the disclosure of a new truth of beings, as they come into being as their new appearance—a new truth of being, having the character of phusis, a whooshing up, a radiance and presence, just as nature once did for the early Greeks, just as science did for the early Scholastics.

A decision must be made!

Fountain Mouth

I want to give a sense of what is at stake in this decision regarding art as originary by reference to one phenomenon occurring in the world today. This phenomenon can go by the name of Slavoj Žižek (he is not the only example)! In case you haven't heard:[23]

> Slavoj Žižek is a Slovenian-born political philosopher and cultural critic. He was described by British literary theorist, Terry Eagleton, as the "most formidably brilliant" recent theorist to

have emerged from Continental Europe.

Žižek's work is infamously idiosyncratic. It features striking dialectical reversals of received common sense; a ubiquitous sense of humor; a patented disrespect towards the modern distinction between high and low culture; and the examination of examples taken from the most diverse cultural and political fields. Yet Žižek's work, as he warns us, has a very serious philosophical content and intention. He challenges many of the founding assumptions of today's left-liberal academy, including the elevation of difference or otherness to ends in themselves, the reading of the Western Enlightenment as implicitly totalitarian, and the pervasive skepticism towards any context-transcendent notions of truth or the good.

I refer you to the Wikipedia entry for the astounding list of books, films, and articles, not to mention the YouTube examples of his talks throughout the world.[24] Although Žižek is well received by many, he has his serious detractors, who are equally scathing and dismissive. One such critic is Noam Chomsky who is dismissive to the point of contempt for Žižek on the grounds of his "non-existent" theorizing. Chomsky disparages Žižek as theorist since Chomsky privileges theorizing as gathering data (facts), calm scientific reasoning, application of principles, carefully argued conclusions etc.

Chomsky's evaluation of Žižek 's work and influence is based entirely on Chomsky's placing his own view of theorizing (and therefore Žižek 's lack of the same) at the centre of his critique. Chomsky is a historian and truth of being lies for him within his chosen *things*—historical documents, and he does not, and cannot, know why Žižek is so influential.

Žižek points out in his rebuttal that Chomsky in fact makes frequent empirical errors. Žižek draws our attention to the Kmer Rouge regime in Cambodia and Chomsky's claim, based on the given facts (documentation), that Kmer Rouge did not represent a threat. When this turned out to be a huge error in judgment, Chomsky said that, at the time, what he said was *true*—meaning that truth laid within the documentation available at the time.[25]

This short summary of the "debate" serves to draw attention to two starkly different possible evaluations of the one phenomenon, "Slavoj Žižek". Chomsky makes his judgment on the basis of what constitutes truth in the metaphysical world—the world of substantial things (and correlative language of reification), the things being historical documents in this case, i.e. stable entities that correlate to "calm reason", theorizing in the established way of science, etc. From this point of view, Žižek, like Hegel's art, can add nothing further to opening the way to this (past) truth.

But, as a phenomenon, Žižek 's mind is an explosion of imagination and ideas! He can barely contain the associations that come pouring in. The way he keeps wiping his nose looks like a cocaine-addiction but probably is a gestural expression of a mind that is working at high revolutions all the time. He is well read enough to draw from fields as diverse as cinema and Hegel. He reminds me of Terrance McKenna. His intellectual scope is breath-taking and yet he does not just lead us into chaos, he always seems to have an Ariadne's thread that keeps him and us linked to the topic. He shakes up calm, measured theorizing and reason and injects new life into closed systems of thought.

One case in point: Žižek claims "anti-Semitism is pathological".[26] Who could remain calm with that provocation? Yet his explanation makes sense: don't accept the discourse (or facts) about anti-Semitism on its own given terms (akin to Einstein saying that a problem cannot be solved on the level of consciousness that gave rise to it in the first place). Pathology turns out to be any discourse that gets frozen in its original terms and therefore cannot advance past its own categories of thought.

In my view Žižek 's cultural influence lies in his amazing ability to break up rigid systems of thought and to inject new life into the discourse, any discourse, setting off new streams of thinking, imagination. This creates movement, fluidity, and destroys encrusted thinking. But he is not just like that great agent of chaos, "The Joker", who says, "Introduce a little anarchy. Upset the established order, and everything becomes chaos. I'm an agent of chaos...." Žižek upsets the given order in a unique, ultimately life-serving way.

Slavoj Žižek is a human representative of the

phenomenon that I call "Fountain-Mouth", after another dream I had around the time of my "Petrified Christ" dream. This phenomenon can only be understood favorably when we have made the decision that Heidegger led us to—art as originating another kind of truth with its corresponding appearances. This consideration gives rise to another question: what is the connection between Fountain-Mouth and the Petrified Christ as an art form?

We can closer to this connection by remembering the Greek myth of Pegasus, born from the gushing blood of the Gorgon, whose stare freezes everything into immobility. This winged horse of inspiration strikes his hoof down into solid rock, releasing the life-giving waters of Hippocrene (horse's fountain). This myth opens the possibility to me that my dream is saying that the living blood of Christ has turned to stone. The flowing blood of the suffering Christ has historically been pictured as *life giving* (the life of the spirit) throughout the centuries. And just now, another detail from my dream has been released into consciousness, as I wrote the previous sentence. In my dream I now remember that the Petrified Christ is shown in the Buddha's lion posture: reclining on his right side, cradling his head in his right hand—at the moment of his death!

You see, this is what "life-giving" may mean today: the petrified Christ alone speaks of death, the end of an age perhaps, the final end of progressive time as a historical narrative—a realization attended by anxiety or maybe even suicidal depression. But the Petrified Christ as an *art work* cracks open the rocks of tradition by showing

Christ in a death pose associated only with the Buddha. Tradition would have Christ die only on the cross.

Attempting to find out what this art work might *mean* would only trap us in those very traditions (e.g. their way of knowing). This dream art work is originary and already has released a stream of new thinking (the thinking that I am now thinking via participation). Understanding in terms of prior categories of thought therefore is not an adequate or relevant response, but rather, to follow the living stream that is released by the dream art work may now just be the "right" way.

My association to Slavoj Žižek was already a response to my dream. It had the same quality as the Buddha association, of my not knowing where it would lead. I followed it anyway and ended up here. To continue, I find a rising river of enthusiasm when I think, "fountain-mouth". Here is the dream that gave me that name:

> … I am now walking naked in a street but turn around to return to home. At home, a marvelous visitor. A cat-headed cassowary bird in iridescent beautiful colors comes in, very friendly, accompanied by small children. He washes or places his head/mouth in a fountain. He and the children are going house-to-house to greet people.

This dream demonstrates the importance of the unexpected detail. In my dream this wonderful being places his mouth in the fountain. The dream wants to bring "mouth" and "fountain" together—fountain-mouth! It wasn't long before I found my way to Rilke and his sonnet from Songs to Orpheus:

> Oh fountain-mouth, you whose gift is always going,
> Inexhaustibly speaking one pure sound—
> You, marble mask before the flowing
> Face of water. And in the far background
> The aqueducts' descent. From far away hills,
> Passing by graves in the Appennines,
> They bring their Saying to you, which then falls
> over the blackened ageing of your tune
> into the basin waiting down below.
> This is the prone and sleeping ear,
> The marble-ear, in which you always speak.
> Earth's ear. So that she's talking here
> To herself alone. Slip a pitcher in the creek
> And it seems to her you interrupt her flow.

The last two lines imply the flow is all-important for Rilke. Quenching our thirst at the spring, or from the blood of Christ, I might add, may belong to another time, another age. Rilke instead became that flow. He flowed! He let the earth speak to him via the ear and through him via his/her fountain-mouth—to herself: an image of the uroborus.

I think Slavoj Žižek is another human representative of a flow that has started up out of the petrified rocks of a long tradition based on Metaphysics and its appearances, where abstractions are perceived (or apperceived) in the world as substantial things—self, cause, effect, law of contradiction, good, evil, inner, outer, matter, etc.—reification!

I now recall another memory from the time I went to India in 1985. I visited Nepal where I attended a talk by the Rinpoche of the White Temple. He pointed to a table and said, "Where is it?" He meant, "Where is the table?" A rather odd question since he was pointing right at the table! He then turned to me in particular and insisted, "Where is it? Is it there or there?" He pointed to various locations in space. Well no, not there or there. So where is it? He pressured me and I became unsure, not knowing what he was getting at. At one point my eyes rolled back momentarily and he burst out in peals of laughter. He had penetrated my habitual mind and he saw that he had done so.

Now, some thirty years later, I have a glimpse of what he was trying to teach me. The kindergarten step required for Buddhist meditation, leading to the final discovery of the nature of mind is such an inquiry as the Rinpoche taught me, not so much in relation to tables, but to the self—that unquestioned substantial thing that we have reified in the West. Rinpoche sought to disturb that easy certainty of selfhood by precise analysis: if the self is a solid thing then where is it? Discovering that the self cannot be found by appeal to the senses, or the imagination, etc. is to understand emptiness, the very first step toward any deeper meditative practices, and a moment of sheer terror![27] Emptiness—the non-substantiality and dependent co-arising of the mind and its productions, usually perceived as independent solid objects in the metaphysical world!

I once had a dream in which I experience the flow that can come out of emptiness:

> I look into the eyes of His Holiness, the Dalia Lama. I encounter emptiness, i.e. the emptiness from which form emerges. I experience a

> moment of terror and then Compassion pours
> out of the emptiness, unending compassion. …

The Coming Guest

C. G. Jung was very concerned about the future—the unknown future. Qualifying the future as "unknown" raises the question how to relate to that kind of future. If you "know" the future (plans, goals, scenarios, trends, predictions, etc.) you can at least go ahead with a commitment of sorts or take your chances with some form of action. But how do you orient to an unknown future? Are you relating to anything at all? Not knowing the future generally awakens uncertainty, terror, a rushing to know. But Jung had none of this in mind when he spoke of the unknown future as an awe-inspiring guest to whom we must extend hospitality, much the same way as Philemon and Baucis welcome their guests (Zeus and Hermes disguised). We extend hospitality to the unknown future when we take up hints, suggestions, unexpected details, chance happenings, and "accidents" —all those events that cannot be safely entombed or petrified in a known category of experience.

When Jung spoke of the unknown future as the "awe-inspiring guest who knocks at our door so portentously", he is speaking poetically, as a mouthpiece of that unknown future, in much the same way that Rilke speaks as the mouthpiece, Fountain-Mouth. It is the *other* that is doing the speaking, through and *as* its human representative. Listen to Leonard Cohen who is now near the end of his life and is thus able to write:[28]

I love to speak with Leonard
He's a sportsman and a shepherd
He's a lazy bastard
Living in a suit

But he does say what I tell him
Even though it isn't welcome
He will never have the freedom
To refuse

He will speak these words of wisdom
Like a sage, a man of vision
Though he knows he's really nothing
But the brief elaboration of a tube

In these succinct lines we are hearing the other in Cohen speak and tell us about the man who has been the mouthpiece of his master, as musician and poet.

Art as poetry, in the way that Heidegger means, is originary speech and poetic speech is the only speech that can bring the new appearances into actuality. Jung wrote of the guest in a letter and he also "spoke" it in a very strange bas-relief carved in the last few years of his life on the wall at Bollingen. Of all Jung's art works, written, carved, or painted, this one has received least attention.29 It resists any interpretation that tries to locate it within any traditional category of thought that would simply petrify it into "knowledge":30

Jung's description of how the bas-relief came into being reveals that, like Cohen, he opened himself to the *other* within who "spoke", this time in images appearing in the rock face. Jung rendered these images into visibility and when they "moved" (i.e. transformed) he followed obediently, participating in the flow and subordinating any desire to "know". As an augur of the future, or as an originary art work, Jung's bas-relief invites further art work that resonates with it and continues to "incarnate" the unknown future through these hints and suggestions. My book, The Coming Guest and the New Art Form is such an attempt.[31]

One detail in Jung's enigmatic carving continues to this day to intrigue and "pull" me since I first paid attention to it—"the bear starts the ball rolling". Jung associated that bear to Russia. At the time I first saw the bas-relief I had been inundated with powerful and compelling dreams that linked my path to "Russia" and (as?) the unknown future.[32] Recently I re-discovered the cinematic work of Russian director Andrey Tarkovsky. To make a long story short, I rushed to purchase his autobiography, Sculpting in Time, sure that I had discovered another thread to the weaving begun by Jung's carving and amplified by my dreams. Here is a small sample of how Tarkovsky thinks:[33]

> When I speak of poetry I'm not thinking of it as a genre. Poetry is an awareness of the world, a particular way of relating to reality. ... such an artist can discern the lines of the poetic design of being. He is capable of going beyond the limitations of coherent logic, and conveying the deep complexity and truth of the impalpable connections and hidden phenomena of life.

If this thought represents the "Russia" that sets the ball rolling, then we can see immediately that the Coming Guest as Fountain-Mouth has something to do with a particular awareness of the world that, like Yeats' beast, is slouching towards Bethlehem to be born, or perhaps, like my cassowary-cat, simply arriving at the door one day, accompanied by children.

---

[1] W. Giegerich: Soul-Violence. Spring Journal Books. New Orleans. 2008, 46.

[2] In early Greek times, natural objects in their *being*, were experienced as *phusus*, a "whooshing up," appearing, and a dying away, once fulfilled. Dreams have the same phenomenology, leaving an imprint as memory, which is then stabilized by repetition.

[3] Physiognomy has a venerable history but has no place in the scientific mind that privileges material causes. When soul and body were better understood as correlative, then the form of the "physical" was understood as being caused by soul (i.e., formal cause—Aristotle).

[4] Owen Barfield: "Matter, Imagination and Spirit" in The Rediscovery of Meaning. San Rafael. The Barfield Press, 1977, 172.

[5] See my book, Overcoming Solidity: World Crisis and the New Nature for a fuller discussion. See www.amazon.com/author/johncwoodcock

[6] Note: Morpheus is the god of dreams. A record of my own experiences of this "melting" may also be found in my book, The Imperative. See www.amazon.com/author/johncwoodcock

[7] I explore the relationship between consciousness and appearances more deeply in my book, Overcoming Solidity.

[8] Heidegger: The Origin of the Work of Art.

[9] By equating "world" with "age", I am saying that the past, present, and future are also understood, along with things, in a certain way characteristic of the world to which they belong. So, for the Christian age, past, present and future are understood as historical, and linear, and from 15th C., *progressive*, quite different from an understanding of time as cyclical or eternal.

[10] W. H. Auden: The 20th century as the Age of Anxiety.

[11] Dante: Inferno. Canto XXXIV.

[12] Ibid: Paradiso. Canto II.

[13] Ibid. Canto XXXIV.

[14] Heidegger: The Age of the World Picture.

[15] Emerson: Nature.

[16] Wolfgang Giegerich: "Fabrication of Time" in Technology of the Soul. Spring Publications. New Orleans. 2007.

[17] C/f the Greek *phusis* for example.

[18] W. Giegerich. Technology and the Soul. 144.

[19] Ibid. 146.

[20] Heidegger: The Origin of the Work of Art. 50 ff.

[21] Ibid. 47.

[22] Irrelevant because Hegel has already thought out the entire age of Metaphysics. There is nothing to add to his thought re: the metaphysical world.

[23] http://www.iep.utm.edu/zizek/

[24] https://en.wikipedia.org/wiki/Slavoj_Žižek_bibliography

[25] All this according to Žižek. See https://www.youtube.com/watch?v=JWOI0Xym2ZY

[26] https://www.youtube.com/watch?v=PIPjmmmh_os

[27] The five aggregates of the sentient being: material form, feelings, perception, volition (sometimes translated as mental formations), and sensory consciousness.

[28] Leonard Cohen (2012): "Going Home" in Old Ideas. http://www.songlyrics.com/leonard-cohen/going-home-lyrics/#HcHQIieyPCiqwZ0D.99

[29] An exceptional discussion of this carving in its character as an augury can be found in R. Lockhart: Psyche Speaks. Chiron. Wilmette. 1982. My book, The Coming Guest also is an "artistic" response to this art work.

[30] Jung tried to interpret the work when requested, but admitted the difficulty. See my book, The Coming Guest and the New Art Form (2nd ed.) at www.amazon.com/author/johncwoodcock

[31] See: http://www.amazon.com/author/johncwoodcock

[32] See my essay, "From Dream to World" in Living in Uncertainty Living with Spirit. www.amazon.com/author/johncwoodcock

[33] Andrey Tarkovsky: Sculpting in Time. University of Texas Press. Austin. 1987, 21.

F INALE: Worlds in Collision

My last essay is a portion of my doctoral dissertation which was written in a dithyrambic furor.[1] The entirety of the piece poured out over a ten-day period. It is in fact a record of the process of breakdown of categories as reflected in my psyche, towards becoming a mouthpiece for the unknown future. You will see inner/outer, dream/reality, subject/object dualities melt away as I heated up from the onslaught of living language. It is virtually unedited from the time of that ten-day "explosion"! I hope you can perceive within the breakdown in syntax as it occurs, an "*other*", a new voice emerging from the chaos.

Living in the world of the Cartesian paradigm I know that matter is on the outside and spirit is in the inside and that they have an abyss between them. These realities are axiomatic, testable and absolute.

> that is until they break down
> until i break down
> until the world breaks up
> when what is so solid crumbles and dissolves
> when what is so ethereal gains flesh and sinew
> solve et coagulatio

Our tragedy today is a general and universal physical fear so long sustained that we are used to it . . . [we] must forget it forever, leaving no room for anything but the old verities and truths of the heart.[2]

> Are you afraid of weakening my son? Are you afraid of that sweet fire? From fixity to fluidity you go.
> Let it go! Let it go! Let it go!
> i am dissolving father
> i am flowing to the sea
> i am mingling with another
> as the sand swirls on the clear bottom
> of a wading pool
> cicadas thrumming through the night
> edges reaching out across space—touching
> they cannot help vibrating
>   we cannot help vibrating
>   iandyou vibrating
>   resonating youandi
>   last drop falling falling falling
> gone!

I am sitting at a table. A huge wind begins to buffet me. I start shaking as it gets stronger. I reach out and grab our mani stone and begin to chant "Om Mani Padme Hum" as the wind reaches a crescendo. I hear in the background a group of Tibetan monks supporting me, chanting too. My body starts up a vibration and I realize that the wind is going through my body. It must be a subtle wind! Startling thought! Or, equally startling, has my body changed to become more transparent to the wind? My experience demands the presence of ambiguity.

Head getting hot when I do too much! My skin breaking out again and burning, burning from the inside! My god! I look sunburned and my face is peeling like a snake shedding its skin. I haven't been outside for weeks on end. Electricity popping my ears and drying out my nose! I feel like a fuse will blow in my third eye. I can't cool down.

I am being initiated by Native Americans . . . the only white man. A ceremonial sacrifice is taking place in which we are placed on the cross and receive cuts on the face and genital. I am also talking with the ancestors who are asking to be released by me. They are trapped. I gain a flash of insight—they seek release into modern incarnation. This holy scene is taking place in the temple of a local garbage dump, the attending priests are tramps, and their holy raiments are ill fitting rags, the sacred objects of veneration are bottles, cans and a gum wrapper lying on the filthy ground with trash, bits and pieces . . . and now I am taken to the Master:

He is a crippled, blind, black man sitting twisted and warped in an old broken wheelchair. His face is the sweet union of a man and a boy. Now I understand how the deformed heal through direct experience of the deformity. I ask, seeking an oracle from him, "will I live now, what is my future?"

He is seated and I sit at his feet in the dust and kiss his foot tenderly, even familiarly, as if we know each other. He smiles, in love, a feeling of equals. He shows me an oracle, my astrology chart, and the houses I have dealt with in this life, and the houses I will deal with in the next. His message is one of love: "Love has broken through in you! You will be all right!" I feel the love, and I go sit in a cafeteria and weep tears of love spontaneously.

When the master loves you, you must die!

I am in my room and I see a door form on the floor. I press on it with my hands. No longer solid but a spongy matter and as I push through the black depths open up and I am dying. I am terrified to go down and I hear thumping below. I also hear the door open and close as alternately I began to relax and fear sets in. My heart is pounding. I remember the countless times I made a temporary descent until I could see something and then I would pop back up with an idea, an image etc. Now I will just go further down. I choose to descend into the abyss and I will not fight it this time. And as I do so, I become blind.

My head is at an awkward angle on the chair. There is a disturbance outside. A bat has landed on the deck, looking directly in. Some black dogs may be chasing him. I struggle to sit upright but my neck muscles are paralyzed. I can't lift my head.

Dr. Jung, as an old man, is in the other chair. People are coming to visit him, while I am sitting on the floor. I ask him about whether he has thought about the point at which psyche or spirit becomes matter (or words become physiological). As I ask I receive an answer from within me: that is the function of the symbol! Simultaneously, Jung nods, "I have and it just so." I relax. He gets up to receive others and strolls into the backyard as I ponder his teaching: how to see in the dark, through vibrations—images formed from sound rather than images formed by light.

The serpent comes, watching me silently from the floor. I close my eyes and remain still. The cobra flicks his tongue in and out of my mouth. As he does so, I feel an indescribable feeling of being loved. Then, he leaves.

I feel the serpent rise up my spine, taking over my body—the cobra! I feel his presence within me and outside of me, his huge hood erect and his head and mine concurrent, his tongue and mine one. Yet I feel separate, a witness in awe yet unafraid. His presence is inexorable; I am his vessel and a willing one. I am the medium through whom he works. He sees through my eyes—implacable irresistible hypnotic fate! Head bends over the woman's foot. Tongue touches her leg and there is a flash of light! Her wound is healed. Withdrawing and I leave once again as ordinary as before.

A huge Grizzly bear embraces me from behind. I feel him so close. Such immense power! I can smell him. I cannot flee. He could crush me. We fall asleep together. I gingerly lift a great paw and slide out. As I leave I realize I have left the bear in the house! I start to doubt my actions. Is my fear at the expense of others' safety? I am so sick of being afraid. I return to him and slide back into his embrace. Now I cannot move without taking Grandfather bear into account.

Now I meet Black Elk and another man. Black Elk has decided to speak and I am very moved by his eloquence. He uses modern psychological language to my great surprise. He says he is no longer going to hold back.

I am beginning to see things that I have not seen before. It's like I have penetrated a veil and can now see how people are behind ethical codes, surface behaviors etc. What people actually are doing in their lives compared with what they are saying they are doing. I have received so much condemnation for my own actions that I have not seen others' shadows. Now I am beginning to and I feel disoriented and unstable. My attention is shifted to the bear and what he wants; that is, my concerns are no longer centered on my ego. There is a duality in my life now.

To be in the bear's embrace is to be alive to the moment, the twist and sudden turns, little predictability. I need to take account of the animal spirit in my actions from now on.

The lion approaches and I become him and he becomes me. I can taste his/my fur on my tongue. Pungent scent fills nostrils. Loping along on the Savannah in easy long strides. Natives, people with dogs are coming. Casually, no fear, claws dig into bark and muscular thighs push up into the crackling branches of a dry tree. Dog comes, slips, yelps in fear and pain, and crashes down. The men come. They are talking about the lion, teaching the young ones about fear. Yellow eyes watch unblinking and rough tongue idly licks an immense paw of power.

I am with an old man from India. It is night, in his bed. I feel some quivering in my abdomen. It is the same quiver I feel every day now. It literally shakes my body like a spring, often forcing a shout out! I close my eyes and make a decision to surrender totally to this old man.

As soon as I do, I faintly hear him say, "Yes the chrysalis is cracking." Now, I know I have become a butterfly, totally.

I now become in body, totally, an eagle. I can fly though like the butterfly dream, it feels new and strange. Wings stretching, stroking the air slowly and cautiously, gliding …

My descent is initiating me into the mystery of image. "Visual" images i.e. based on the eyes with metaphors of light produce an image as object, disembodied and always over there. I see a lion—the Cartesian paradigm—subject and object split. I and the lion, self and other forever apart! And so my capacity to see this way was blinded in my descent where Jung offers a teaching and then the Serpent, Bear, Lion, Butterfly, and Eagle.

Images based on the other senses: ear, tongue, skin, nose, fingers—sensual images—these images gain body and spirit materializes! And worlds begin to interpenetrate, subject to subject.

I am lying in bed and I feel the familiar deep shudders

inside. I decide to go with them, not to wake up and I succeed. I can lift off the bed. At first there is a short period of darkness in which I could not see. Then I could see the bed, below. I am up in the corner of the room looking down. There is a film on my eyes, like tears partially cleared but I can see perfectly. I touch the ceiling and find it soft and crumbly as if I could go through it but I decide not to do that out of fear. There is an old light bulb and old decorations on the ceiling. "What are they doing there? That's different from what is normally there!" But as evidence, I decided to unscrew the bulb and bring it down with me. I push off the ceiling and again there is a period of darkness and I am in bed again. I try to talk but I am curiously paralyzed. With an effort of will I jerk awake.

I feel the buzzing vibrations that seem to signal a shift in reality. Is this the insect storm? I feel fear and then let it go. I notice my hand is penetrating the bed/earth and scooping through it. Matter has become more fluid, as I have experienced before. I push my face through the bed. I can see. Some effort is needed but the solidity gives way to a more fluid matter. I feel I can, if I dare, go through the wall into my neighbor's apartment. Lack of fear is the key. I felt more ready than ever to do it. But not yet! What if I get stuck? Ahh! Fear prevents the interpenetration and keeps the other out!

Then I am in bed, aware that I am sleeping-yet-awake. I feel something entering that feels dangerous. "Entering" is exactly the right word but "entering where" is the wrong question. If I say it is entering the room then I am in the Cartesian Paradigm with its certainty of what is inside and what is outside. "Entering me" is more like it as long as I stay ambiguous about the meaning of "me."

The animal enters me and moves into a crouch position on the bed. Rippling power arcing through chest. Mouth elongates with teeth sharp and bared. A low basso growl utters easily, vibrantly deep inside. A crouch that could spring into instantaneous explosive violence! I can feel the full sensual reality of the animal. Then a kind of magnetic field places an iron grip around my ankles, like hands pulling my feet from the crouch position out horizontally behind me so that my feet are suspended in the wall. Mastering a sudden spasm of fear, I experiment. I push and pull, and the force resists like a magnet. I become determined this time to go through the wall and not be held back by fear like the last time. I push and push until I go through and I finally am on the outside of my apartment, above the ground.

I descend slowly to the ground and begin to walk around seeing if it was all the same as in the daytime. Yes, but not quite. Then I develop the feeling that I might be making this up, i.e. a doubt, and it becomes more dreamlike and, simultaneously, I return to my body, awake with the memory quite intact.

At last I went through matter. The animal helped me do it—of course! Fear keeps subject and object apart. The animal gave me courage. When my humanness is interpenetrated with the animal, spirit and matter interpenetrate—matter loses its impenetrability and spirit gains body. The wild animal body is the key to the new paradigm!

The image as animal—the key to the new paradigm! What did Jung say? "Why have the animals disappeared from the Christian teaching? When animals are no longer included in the religious symbol or creed, it is the beginning of the dissociation between religion and nature. Then there is no mana in it. As long as the animals are there, there is life in the symbol; otherwise, the beginning of the end is indicated."

In my experiences, image as animal is recovered. I experienced image in full sensual reality. It emerged into ordinary reality through my own senses. I became other and other entered embodied existence through me—an interpenetration of worlds!

A low basso growl rumbles easily from my lips and I have become a mouthpiece for other who enters me in order to become conscious in this world. And so a world is destroyed—a world in which self and other are separated by an abyss—and a new world is becoming through an interpenetration of realities. He comes; he fills my every cell with his presence and he speaks; and thus enters existence, conscious. I am shaken to the core and when he leaves, my body is a trembling leaf. When he leaves I am returned to my familiar world of duality ... or am I?

My memory of our encounter is so clear—a full sensual memory! A memory of his smell, the texture of his fur, the easy magnificent power in his body, the memory of his perception of this world. An echo of the image as animal remains with me. A door to his consciousness remains open through this memory. I know I can find my way back there again, with even less fear than before. If called I will answer for I feel a growing obligation in me to do so—Neruda's obligation:

> To whoever is not listening to the sea
> this Friday morning, to whoever is cooped up
> in house or office, factory or woman
> or street or mine or dry prison cell,
> to him I come, and without speaking or looking
> I arrive and open the door of his prison,
> and a vibration starts up, vague and insistent,
> a long rumble of thunder adds itself
> to the weight of the planet and the foam,
> the groaning rivers of the ocean rise,
> the star vibrates quickly in its corona
> and the sea beats, dies, and goes on beating.

Two worlds collide—such generative violence—and there is a becoming. "Life at the core is steel on stone" from which emerges the new form.[3] What we call art is a palpable echo of two galaxies slowly winding through each other over millennia tearing their cells apart with the cosmic force of love yet holding their integrity with spirallic majesty, forever able to carry the memory of that great encounter.

My obligation is generated by the pressing down on me of a galaxy:[4]

> Press down hard on me, break in
> that I may know the weight of your hand,
> and you, the fullness of my cry.

I am wax upon which the great seal has impressed itself, and thus I am forever changed. The scars I bear in my body are the tattoos prompting memory, entering which I may sing and in so singing a vibration may start up so that you may see a storm on the horizon coming towards you in the heat of a noon day sun. Your nostrils may flair with a sudden inhalation of dust and the musky sour scent of the power of "cool unlying life rushing into your blood".[5] With a start you may realize that you do not know if you are afraid or beginning to brim with a strange excitement. Quickening, you do not know whether to run or to hold out your arms in a wild embrace of the *other* who now descends upon you with the passion and ferocity of immediate compelling presence—your own presence—and you will not know whether you are "a bird, a storm or a great song!"[6]

> How many flowers fail in wood or perish in the hills without the privilege to know that they are beautiful?[7]

one
i burst forth to greet you, in a paroxysm of joy
yet how often are you gone
i wither and die: where are you?
my sorrow turns to the dank deep earth
i descend slowly
until i meet a surging upwelling of joy
catching me in its wake forcing me
to break forth once more with a silent shout
throwing the doors of my colors wide open
once more to your embrace

two
come, mate with me! make honey!

three
one stray kiss from you thrown carelessly
as you force your way through trees
is enough to gladden me
to ecstasy!

four

why do you rush so, great one?
linger with me.my face will follow yours forever
and when you pass
i will wilt and wither
fade and die

five

what do i want from you?
only this ...
gaze upon me with all the violence of your desire
until i know who i am in your eyes.

six

you are leaving now. yes, i can feel it
you are returning to your restless wanderings
while i remain, my veils in disarray
was it worth it - this all too brief liaison, great god?
i know i touched you
before you withdrew
into your silent passage above

---

[1] I completed my PhD in 1999.

[2] W. Faulkner.

[3] C. G. Jung.

[4] Rilke.

[5] D. H. Lawrence.

[6] Rilke.

[7] E. Dickinson.

A BOUT THE AUTHOR

I hold a doctorate in Consciousness Studies (1999). My thesis concerns the theme of "the end of the world", based on my own personal experiences lasting twenty years. At first it seemed to me that I was undergoing a purely personal psychological crisis but over time I discovered that I was also participating in the historical process of a transformation of the soul, as reflected in the enormous, even apocalyptic, changes occurring in our culture. During this difficult period of my life, I wrote two books: Living in Uncertainty Living with Spirit and Poems of Making, Poems of Death, as I tried to give voice to the meaning of my experiences.

My next three books, Mouthpiece, The Imperative, and Hearing Voices, explore the meaning of "the end of the world" more fully. My subsequent books, including Animal Soul and Manifesting Possible Futures, establish a firm theoretical ground for the claim that the soul is urging us towards the development of new inner capacities that can help us face the uncertainty of modern life and, as well, address the unknown future.

My book, Overcoming Solidity, continues this exploration in terms of our current structure of consciousness and its correlative world of empirical reality. Making New Worlds begins the work of articulating an art form that is emerging in response to the unknown future. I develop this theme more fully in The Coming Guest and the New Art Form. I have also written an unusual book, UR-image, which tells a story of four friends whose lives are interrupted by an intrusion of four possible futures, while Oblivion of Being is a story of three friends participating in a transformation of being.

A preview of all my books is available on YouTube:

https://youtu.be/DKfiR_K5nps, or you can visit:

http://www.amazon.com/author/johncwoodcock

I currently live in Sydney with my wife, Anita Hansen, where I teach, write, and consult with others concerning their own journey through the present "apocalypse of the interior", as it has been called, in my capacity as a practicing Jungian psychotherapist. Anita and I also work with couples in a therapeutic setting.

Contact: jwoodcock@lighthousedownunder.com